AF600516

THE CATHOLIC UNIVERSITY OF AMERICA
CANON LAW STUDIES
Number 73

THE PASCHAL PRECEPT

AN HISTORICAL SYNOPSIS AND COMMENTARY

A DISSERTATION

Submitted to the Faculty of Canon Law of the Catholic University of America in Partial Fulfillment of the Requirements for the Degree of

DOCTOR OF CANON LAW

BY

REV. CONNELL CLINTON, A.B., J.C.L.,
Priest of the Archdiocese of Philadelphia

THE CATHOLIC UNIVERSITY OF AMERICA
WASHINGTON, D. C.
1932

Nihil Obstat:

VALENTINUS SCHAAF, O.F.M., J.C.D.,
Censor Deputatus.

Washingtonii, D. C., die XIV Aprilis, 1932.

Imprimatur:

DIONYSIUS CARDINALIS DOUGHERTY,
Archiepiscopus Philadelphiensis.

Philadelphiae, die XV Aprilis, 1932.

Printed by
THE PAULIST PRESS
New York, N. Y.

TO MY FATHER AND MOTHER

TABLE OF CONTENTS

CHAPTER V

FOREWORD

Although there are undoubtedly many questions of greater importance in the field of Canon Law, the question of the paschal precept has much to recommend it as a topic for research and commentary. For the most part, commentators on the Code of Canon Law give but meagre attention to this subject, reserving and directing their study to other more important questions; very often they content themselves with a mere paraphrase of the canons. It was the desire to present a complete though concise survey of the present legislation on the obligatory reception of Communion once a year, as well as a keen interest in the field of eucharistic legislation in general, which prompted the choice of the topic for this monograph.

A word must be said concerning the historical synopsis of the legislation preceding the Code. The present prescriptions of the law contain little which is new. To be understood, they must be studied under the circumstances which caused their enactment. To take a canon from its historical environment is to divorce a text from its context. On the other hand, it is impossible to present a detailed and critical history within the limits of one chapter.

The writer takes this occasion to express his gratitude to the Faculty of Canon Law for their interest and assistance, to Rev. James J. O'Rourke, A.B., J.C.L., for many valuable suggestions, to Rev. Delisle Lemieux, M.A., J.C.L., for assistance in preparing the proofs, and to all those who have cooperated in the preparation of this study.

CHAPTER I

THE NECESSITY OF COMMUNION

It is customary for theologians, in harmony with many of the Fathers of the Church, to distinguish three kinds of Communion; the merely sacramental Communion, which produces no effects in the soul of the recipient because of mortal sin; the spiritual Communion, which is nothing else than the pious desire to receive the Blessed Eucharist; and finally the Communion which is at one and the same time sacramental and spiritual, received by a soul which is in the state of grace. Undoubtedly it was this last species of Communion which Christ had in mind when He delivered His famous discourse on the Eucharist at Capharnaum. It was in this sermon that Jesus declared that the reception of His Body and Blood was a necessary condition for salvation. This is the natural inference to be drawn from His words—"Amen, amen I say to you: Except you eat the flesh of the Son of Man, and drink His Blood, you shall not have life in you." [1] It is not surprising, then, that the Fathers make participation in the Eucharist the indispensable condition of the supernatural life within the soul, and of the glorious resurrection of the body.[2] In the last analysis one must have recourse to these words of our Saviour to prove the necessity whether of divine law or ecclesiastical, of receiving the Body and Blood of Christ as food and drink for the soul.

The principal purpose of the present dissertation is to discuss the question of the necessity of receiving the Eucharist only in so far as it has been determined by ecclesiastical authority. Consequently it does not enter within the purview of this study to establish a dogmatic or moral thesis, such as the dogma of the Real Presence, or an obligation, based on the divine law, of receiving Communion a certain number of times during life. Its object is merely to trace the evolution of the present ecclesiastical precept of Easter Com-

[1] John, VI, 54.

[2] Labauche, *The Three Sacraments of Initiation*, p. 381.

munion, and in the latter part of the dissertation, to interpret the final expression of the Church's attitude towards the obligatory reception of Communion as found in the Code of Canon Law in the light of this historical-canonical development. Yet a brief consideration on the necessity of the Eucharist will not be without value since the whole *raison d'être* of the paschal precept is founded on the relation of man's eternal salvation to the reception of Communion. This fact is in itself sufficient justification for a preliminary discussion of the necessity of Communion in general.

ARTICLE I.—COMMUNION IS NOT NECESSARY *Necessitate Medii*

One must distinguish two kinds of necessity: first the necessity of means, *necessitas medii,* and secondly, the necessity of precept, or *necessitas praecepti.* In the first case, a thing or action is necessary by necessity of means when without it a given end cannot be obtained:—the eye, for example, is necessary for vision. The second kind of necessity is that which is imposed by the free will of a superior, for example, the necessity of fasting. As regards the Eucharist a further distinction must be made between infants and adults. It is quite simple to prove that in the case of infants the Eucharist is not necessary for salvation by necessity of precept, for obviously, since they have not as yet obtained the use of reason, they are free from the obligation of positive laws. Consequently, in regard to children, the only question is whether Communion like Baptism is necessary for them as a means of salvation.[3]

The Holy Eucharist, wonderful gift of God as it is, is not held by the Catholic Church to be a sacrament which is necessary *necessitate medii* for salvation. That is, absolutely speaking, the soul of man can attain the Beatific Vision even if Communion has never been received during life. Theologians teach that all that is necescary for admission to the bliss of heaven is the sanctifying grace of our most Holy Redeemer; and this can be conferred by Baptism, by the sacrament of Penance, or even, under certain circumstances, by acts of contrition alone. In opposition to this doctrine, a few Greek schismatics and some theologians of the Reformed Church held that

[3] Pohle-Preuss, *The Sacraments,* II, 236.

the Holy Eucharist was necessary *necessitate medii.*[4] Exaggerating the necessity of the Eucharist as a means to salvation, Rosmini advanced the untenable opinion that at the moment of death this heavenly food is supplied in the next world to children who had just departed this life. This view was formally condemned by Leo XIII.[5] The Council of Trent had virtually rejected it in advance when it declared "Parvulos usu rationis carentes *nulla* obligari necessitate ad sacramentalem Eucharistiae communionem."[6]

The custom in the early Church of giving Communion to children does not weaken this conclusion. It is true that from the third to the eleventh century the Latin Church administered the Eucharist to infants under the species of wine immediately after Baptism and Confirmation, as is still the custom among the Orientals. But here theory and practice must be carefully distinguished. The Church did not introduce this custom because she believed that infants could not be saved without Holy Communion. For instance, she never held that the sacrament of Confirmation was necessary for salvation, yet she administered, and still administers in some places, this sacrament to infants. Moreover, the Council of Trent declared that the custom of the primitive Church of giving Communion to children was not based upon the erroneous belief of its necessity to salvation, but upon the circumstances of the times.[7]

Since it is an article of faith that children are not obliged by necessity of means to receive the Eucharist, *a fortiori,* Communion is not necessary *necessitate medii* for adults. This conclusion, although not *de fide,* is at least theologically certain.

Article II.—Communion Is Necessary *Necessitate Praecepti*

Although Communion is not necessary by necessity of means, it is necessary, both by divine and ecclesiastical precept for all the faithful who have reached the age of reason. In the first place, one

[4] Lupi, *La SS. Eucaristia,* p. 209; Pohle-Preuss, *l. c.*

[5] *Prop. Rosmini damn. a Leone XIII,* die 14 Dec. 1887; prop. 32—D. B., n. 1922.

[6] Sess. XXI, *de communione,* cap. 4—D. B., n. 933.

[7] *Ibid.*

may take it as certain that there is some obligation arising from the divine law of receiving the sacrament of the Eucharist.[8] One cannot but see a divine command in these words of Our Lord: "Unless you eat the flesh of the Son of Man and drink His Blood, you shall not have life in you."[9] This text must be understood in its obvious sense of the sacramental reception of the Body and Blood of Christ.[10] In conditioning eternal life upon the reception of the Eucharist, Our Lord clearly intended to give a strict command. Besides, He added a grave sanction to this mandate, namely, the privation of supernatural life, the corollary of which is eternal damnation. The Council of Trent plainly intimates that a divine command was given because it teaches that "Christ commanded His followers to honour His memory by Communion."[11] A further argument may be deduced from the words which follow the institution of the Eucharist, namely, "Do this in commemoration of Me."[12] This text has always been interpreted by tradition of the obligation, not only of offering the unbloody Sacrifice of the Mass, but also of the Eucharist, because Christ ordered that to be done by His Church which had been done at the last Supper. In the last Supper, however, besides the oblation of the Body and Blood of Christ, the Apostles received Holy Communion. Consequently, since the pronomen *hoc* indicates the whole action taken substantially, it is legitimate to infer that Christ laid down a precept for the reception of the Eucharist.[13]

Suarez[14] proves the existence of a divine precept also from another angle. The Eucharist, he argues, is a spiritual food and drink, and just as material food and drink are necessary for the conservation of the natural life, so also the Eucharist is necessary for the preservation of the supernatural life. It is, moreover, in the ordinary

[8] Gasparri, *Tractatus Canonicus de SS. Eucharistia,* n. 1142.

[9] John, VI, 54.

[10] Gasparri, *op. cit.*, n. 1142; Rosset, *Theologia Dogmatica-Moralis, de Eucharistia,* n. 874.

[11] Sess. XIII, *de instit. ss. Eucharistiae,* cap. 2—D. B., n. 875.

[12] Luke, XXII, 19; I Cor., XI, 25.

[13] Rosset, *op. cit.*, n. 874; Suarez, *Opera Omnia,* XXI, q. LXXX, a. XI, disp. LXIX, sect. I.

[14] *Ibid.*

providence of God, morally necessary for perseverance and salvation. Accordingly, if the Eucharist is not a necessary means for salvation, at least it is a most helpful one. Man, however, is obliged to use not only the means which are indispensable, but also those which might be termed morally necessary for the attaining of his end in life. The natural inference is that man is bound to receive the Eucharist. But this obligation presupposes a precept; consequently it may safely be assumed that Christ gave one. This line of reasoning has also been adopted by St. Thomas.[15] "Through our natural concupiscence," he writes, "and through our being so taken up with external things, there ensues a constant diminishing of that devotion and fervour which should keep us near to God; and therefore it is essential that such loss be frequently made good, or else a man will be wholly alienated from God." But what more potent remedy is there than the Holy Eucharist for making good such loss? which consideration forces him to conclude that man is obliged to receive this Sacrament not only by the law of the Church, but also by the command of Christ Himself.

Although the precept is clearly defined, it is not so evident just how far this obligation is binding. Its gravity may be inferred from the sanction which Christ attached to it, namely, the privation of the eternal reward. Although it binds every man, evidently it does not bind all in the same degree. Its urgency will depend upon many circumstances, on a man's disposition, surroundings and temptations, and on the character of the times in which he lives. The most common opinion holds that the divine precept urges, when a person is in a proximate or probable danger of death.[16] For, granting with Suarez that the Eucharist is at least a relatively and morally necessary means of salvation in the sense that no adult Catholic can sustain his spiritual life if he voluntarily neglects to receive Holy Communion for a long time, surely there is no moment in a man's life when he needs that means more than at the hour of death—that hour when weakness is so great, and temptation is so strong.

Theologians also teach that the divine precept obliges *per se* to the reception of the Eucharist several times during life. This is only

[15] *Summa Theologica*, IV, Dist. 12, q. 3, a. 1, sol. 1.

[16] Labauche, *The Three Sacraments of Initiation*, p. 383.

logical if one stops to consider its nature and purpose. Christ instituted this wonderful Sacrament *per modum panis* for the conservation of the spiritual life, and bread is of its very nature destined for frequent consumption.[17] *Per accidens*, the obligation of receiving Communion would bind a person for whom it would be the sole means of resisting a grave temptation.[18]

Article III.—The Ecclesiastical Precept

Since Christ has left no definite precept as to the frequency with which He desired man to receive Him in the Eucharist, it belongs to the Church to determine the divine command more accurately by prescribing fixed times for the reception of Holy Communion. For this reason, the Church, in order to secure at least a qualified compliance with the command of Christ, has formulated a law by which the faithful are bound to approach the altar at least once a year, and that during what is called the paschal time. It would be a grave mistake, however, to assume for a moment that an annual Communion is the ideal of the Church. Such infrequent reception of the Eucharist as this is not the normal condition of a good Catholic. A careful consideration of the history of Communion leads a modern writer [19] to the conclusion that of the eighteen centuries of the existence of the Church there were only four, the tenth, the eleventh, twelfth, and thirteenth, during which infrequent Communion was the rule, without a visible movement against it, among the persons living in the world. From this survey he deduces that frequent Communion is the normal state of the Church. In the face of this evidence, it is surprising that the Church had to reduce the obligation of receiving the Eucharist to one solitary Communion in the year. Yet such action on her part was not the result of any hasty or ill-conceived planning, but rather the outcome of the particular legislation of several centuries.

In this study it is the writer's intention to give an historical synopsis of the Church's attitude towards the obligatory reception

[17] Rosset, *op. cit.*, n. 888; Tanquerey, *Synopsis Theologiae Dogmaticae*, III, n. 643; Gasparri, *op. cit.*, n. 514.

[18] Tanquerey, *op. cit.*, n. 643; Labauche, *op. cit.*, p. 383.

[19] Dalgairns, *The Holy Communion*, p. 184.

of the Eucharist as reflected in past legislation, before interpreting the final expression of this attitude as found in the Code of Canon Law. It is clear that for the better understanding of any law an inquiry into its origin and its historical development and evolution is of the greatest importance. The value of an historical study of the evolution of the paschal precept is twofold. By acquainting himself with the origin and early legislation on the reception of Communion, the student will be the better prepared to appreciate the force of the laws in existence at the present time. Secondly, canon 6, § 1, 2, prescribes that "the ancient legislation which has been incorporated into the new law without any or with but verbal changes, retains its former binding force and will have to be interpreted in the same sense as it was interpreted in the past by approved authors. Some of the ancient laws have entered into the new canons with modifications; these canons have to be understood in the light of the ancient law in so far as they agree with it." [20] Since the former legislation on the reception of the Eucharist substantially coincides with the present dispositions of the Code, a brief historical excursus is not only desirable but necessary.

[20] Ayrinhac, *General Norms,* p. 106.

CHAPTER II

LEGISLATION BEFORE THE CODE

ARTICLE I.—PRELIMINARY SURVEY

BEFORE the Fourth Council of the Lateran in 1215, there was no universal ecclesiastical law obliging the faithful to receive Communion during the paschal season. However, throughout the more than a thousand years which elapsed from the institution of the Church to the thirteenth century, a great diversity of custom and precept is to be found, some requiring frequent reception of Communion, others allowing a minimum observance. At no time throughout this entire period is it possible to find absolute uniformity, nor did this obtain until the promulgation of the famous Lateran decree. It is a far cry from the first five centuries of the Church's existence to the golden period of her glory, and one is justified in asking why a study of the Easter Communion should include an article on the period when she did not have to resort to legislation to compel the faithful to obey Christ's injunction. It is an accepted principle in philosophy that every effect has a cause. This same principle of causality may very well be applied here. The Easter Communion became obligatory for the whole Church in the thirteenth century, it is true, but the causes leading to the promulgation of that precept are to be sought, not in the thirteenth century, but in the sporadic efforts of particular councils to meet the widespread neglect of the faithful in receiving the Eucharist. The ordinance of the Fourth Lateran Council was but the climax of all this legislative activity.

It will be of interest to trace the successive steps of this legislation, a development which is very ably described by Peter of Blois.[1]

In the early Church all who attended the consecration of the elements, communicated. However, when the number of the faithful increased, and it was seen that all did not approach the Holy Table,

[1] Serm. 16—quoted by Benedict XIV, *De Synodo Dioecesana,* lib. V, c. 1, n. 7.

it was ordered that all should communicate at least on Sundays. Again, when the chaff began to choke the good seed, and the love of the faithful began to grow cold, it was decreed that at least on the solemn feasts, namely, Easter, Pentecost, and Christmas, the faithful should receive Communion. Finally, now when evil days are come, and the faithful have turned away from the observance of this law, a custom has been introduced, I dare not say by the precept of the Church, but at least by its tacit permission, of communicating but once in the year.

This summary gives in brief the evolution of the present paschal precept. First, there is the reception of Communion at every Mass. Then the custom of communicating every Sunday becomes prevalent. These two steps, for the purpose of division, may be styled as proper to the first five centuries, although not exclusively. Finding the custom of receiving the Eucharist every Sunday a little too arduous for the ever cooling fervour of the faithful, the discipline was further relaxed, so that the reception of Holy Communion was made obligatory only on the major feasts. In the course of time, even this rather lenient precept became irksome for the large majority of the faithful, so that as a last resource, the Church was compelled to limit the Communion of obligation to a solitary reception in the year.

In the following article it is proposed to trace the evolution of the first step in this evolution, namely, the obligation, if any, of receiving the Eucharist in the first five centuries.

Article II.—The Obligation of Receiving the Eucharist During the First Five Centuries

§ 1. *The Apostolic Period*

It seems quite certain that all who assisted at the eucharistic sacrifice in apostolic times received Holy Communion.[2] Some go a step further in seeking to discover an obligation to receive the Eucharist at these eucharistic gatherings. For example, Rauschen,[3]

[2] Ferraris, *Bibliotheca* v. *"Eucharistia,"* art. I, n. 108; Benedict XIV, *De Synodo Dioecesana,* lib. VII, c. XII, n. 6; Corblet, *Histoire du Sacrement del' Eucharistie,* I, 349; Gasparri, *Tractatus Canonicus de SS. Eucharistia,* II, 377.

[3] *Eucharist and Penance,* p. 135.

holds that it was incumbent upon all baptized Christians to partake of the eucharistic sacrifice when they assisted at the service unless prevented by penitential discipline. In this opinion he is supported by such considerable authorities as Vasquez and Bingham. Bingham goes even so far as to say that an ecclesiastical censure was attached to the violation of this obligation, for he writes:

> Whence it is evident that the most ancient and primitive custom was for all who were allowed to stay, to communicate in the participation of the Eucharist also, except only the last class of penitents, who were admitted to hear the prayers, but not to make the oblation or receive the Communion. These only excepted, all other baptized persons were not only permitted, but, by the rules of the Church, obliged to communicate in the Eucharist under pain of ecclesiastical censure.[4]

In spite of these learned authorities, it is difficult to posit the existence of a precept compelling the reception of the Eucharist, since manifestly there was no need of imposing an obligation during the apostolic age because the fervour of the first Christians certainly warranted their receiving Communion at every Mass they attended.[5] Then, again, these authors have not adduced any cogent reasons to support their opinion. According to Corblet,[6] the general obligation of receiving Communion was never specifically determined by a special law for the simple reason affirmed above, namely, that there was no occasion for it on account of the devotion of the early Christians. The custom of frequent reception of the Eucharist dispensed with the necessity of a law. Hence it is more probable that frequent reception of Communion was optional, although welcome and expected by the Church.[7] It is yet to be proved that in any age of the Church mere non-communicants were forbidden to hear Mass, or that the precept of hearing Mass involved the precept of receiving Communion.[8]

[4] *Christian Antiquities*, V, 154.

[5] "Il n'était pas besoin de prescrire aux fideles de recevoir l'eucharistie; la coutume generale alors, de communier tres frequemment, tenait lieu de loi."—Mourou, "Communion Eucharistique," *Dict. De Théol. Cath.*, I, 484; Probst, *Sakramente und Sakramentalien*, p. 236.

[6] *Histoire du Sacrement del' Eucharistie*, I, 351.

[7] Hedley, *The Holy Eucharist*, p. 132.

[8] Bridgett, *A History of the Holy Eucharist in Great Britain*, I, 48.

It is one thing to say that the first Christians communicated every time the Holy Sacrifice took place, but it is quite another to prove that Mass was celebrated daily. There are no documents extant from the first century to prove that daily Communion or daily Mass was the practice of the faithful. St. Paul, it must be admitted, wrote: "When you come, therefore, together into one place, it is not now to eat the Lord's Supper."[9] In this place he is talking of the Agape which accompanied the celebration of the Mysteries, and he supposes the fact of the faithful communicating every time they come together, but he fails to give any indication of the frequency of these reunions.[10] Consequently, whether the Eucharistic Sacrifice was celebrated daily in the first Christian communities, as has so often been assumed, is open to grave doubt. It is difficult to prove it from the New Testament [11] although some endeavour to show it from a description given in the Acts of the Apostles. In the second chapter of the Acts [12] it is related how "they were persevering in the breaking of bread and in prayers," and in another place in the same chapter [13] that they were "continuing daily with one accord in the temple and breaking bread from house to house." Rauschen [14] thinks that it would be logical to infer from these texts that the early Christians celebrated the Eucharist daily. Yet on a close examination of the text, this inference would depend on whether *daily* applies to the whole verse or the first clause only. It must be admitted that within the walls of Jerusalem, the early Christians led a life much like that of a religious order, inasmuch as they held property in common and were occupied in almost incessant prayer.[15] But whether they celebrated Mass every evening remains uncertain. Granting that it was, it soon ceased to be a rite which was performed after every evening meal. The business of daily life in both Jewish and Christian communities of the Dispersion was too

[9] I Cor. XI, 20.

[10] Dublanchy, "Communion Eucharistique," *Dict. de Théol. Cath.*, I, 516.

[11] Döllinger, *The First Age of Christianity and the Church,* p. 336.

[12] II, 42.

[13] II, 46.

[14] *Eucharist and Penance,* p. 135.

[15] Fouard, *St. Paul and His Missionary Journeys,* p. 184.

exhausting to admit of so frequent religious services as were held in Jerusalem.

§ 2. *Daily Communion in the First Five Centuries*

In the early Church it is impossible to find uniformity in the practice of the different churches in receiving the Eucharist, but as a rule, Communion was received more frequently in the western than in the eastern churches. The question whether daily Communion in the first years of the Church was the practice of the faithful hinges to a large extent on the correlative question of the daily celebration of the Mass. Regarding this latter question, the practice seems to have varied in different regions and at different times.[16] As a consequence, it would be inaccurate to claim that daily Communion was the general custom in the first centuries of the existence of the Church. For instance, it is uncertain whether Mass was publicly celebrated every day in Rome even as late as the time of St. Gregory the Great.[17] In some localities there existed a custom, long since fallen into desuetude, which is of assistance in reconciling the possibility of daily Communion with the lack of a daily Sacrifice. In the earlier years of the Church, the Blessed Sacrament was entrusted with exceeding facility to the faithful to be consumed at home, and this custom was very common during a period of persecution. The moment the Church was declared to be in a state of persecution, the first act of the bishop was to distribute the Sacrament among the faithful that they might take Our Lord to their homes and communicate privately as they pleased.[18] Our Lord set no bounds to the prodigality with which He gave Himself to the faithful in those troubled times, and the Church knew His mind so well that the utmost latitude was then allowed in the conveyance of the Holy Eucharist. Even after the persecutions, this custom was maintained among solitaries in monasteries where there were no priests, and generally among those who lived at a great distance from the Church.[19]

It is almost entirely from the early Christian writers such as St.

[16] Corblet, *op. cit.*, I, 404.

[17] Duchesne, *Christian Worship*, p. 230.

[18] Many, *Praelectiones de Missa*, n. 143; Dalgairns, *The Holy Communion*, p. 191.

[19] Duchesne, *op. cit.*, p. 249.

Justin, Tertullian, Cyprian, Ambrose, Augustine, and Chrysostom, that a knowledge of the customs and time of receiving Communion is learned. The testimony of Tertullian is especially helpful in determining what was the practice with regard to the reception of the Eucharist in Africa. In the course of one of his letters he seems to assume that his readers know of this custom. "Will not your husband know what you taste in secret before all food? and if it appeareth to him to be bread, will he not believe it to be that which is reported?"[20] From this it is reasonable to infer that the faithful were in the habit of taking away with them from the Mass on Sunday small Particles which they preserved at home in the Arca in order that they might communicate on other days.[21] However, it is usually unsafe to draw general conclusions from these isolated instances in the early ecclesiastical writers. It is true, for example, that some of the faithful brought part of the consecrated Host home with them, but it does not follow that this was their regular procedure, or that all observed this custom.[22]

There is some evidence extant which serves to indicate what was the custom of the faithful in Rome with regard to the reception of the Eucharist. St. Jerome, who knew that city as well as he knew Bethlehem, thus replies to an inquirer concerning fasts and Communion.

> You ask me if we should fast on Saturday, and whether the Eucharist should be received daily as the Roman and Spanish Churches are accustomed to. . . . For my part I consider that the traditions of the Church ought to be observed as they have been handed down to us from our ancestors, and that customs introduced by others not in accord with these should be set aside. . . . Let every province abound in its own sense and reverence the precepts of our ancestors as the mandates of the apostles.[23]

These are very strong words in the mouth of St. Jerome. The apostolic tradition was something too sacred to be tampered with;

[20] *Ad Uxor.*, II, 5—*M. P. L.*, I, 1296; Bingham, *Christian Antiquities*, V, 359.

[21] Villien, *A History of the Commandments*, p. 19C.

[22] Corblet, *op. cit.*, I, 404.

[23] *Ep. ad Luc.*,—*M. P. L.*, XXII, 672.

besides he would scarcely have used a phrase which he has employed in proof of some of the fundamental doctrines of Christianity unless he really meant that daily Communion was of apostolic or sub-apostolic origin. Then, again, it may be inferred from this passage that, at the time of the composition of this letter, there was lacking that uniformity of custom in the reception of the Eucharist which was one of the strongest reasons for the promulgation of the Lateran decree.[24]

§ 3. *Sunday Communion*

However much the custom of receiving Communion and of celebrating the Holy Sacrifice varied throughout the Church, at least on the Lord's day it was universally celebrated in all Churches, and never omitted by any assembly of Christians whatsoever. For this reason, among other names, Sunday was anciently called *dies panis* because the breaking of bread was so general a custom in the Church on that day.[25] Even as early as the missionary journeys of St. Paul, the celebration of the Eucharist began to be customary on Sundays only in some parts of the infant Church. For the Apostle admonishes the Corinthians to put aside a small offering on the first day of the week for the Christians at Jerusalem [26] and the Acts of the Apostles relate of his sojourn at Troas that "on the first day of the week, when we were assembled to break bread, Paul discoursed with them. . . . " [27]

The custom of receiving Communion on Sunday was so universal that some writers in their zeal have endeavoured to discover some precept ordering the weekly reception of the Eucharist. In an effort to support this point, some have appealed to the testimony of the Didache, a document which probably belongs either to the last decades of the first century or the early years of the second. In its fourteenth chapter is found the following text:—"Assemble on the Lord's Day, break bread, and give thanks." [28] An unbiassed critic

[24] Rauschen, *Eucharist and Penance*, p. 137.

[25] Bingham, *Christian Antiquities*, V, 358.

[26] I Cor., XVI, 2.

[27] Acts, XX, 7.

[28] Didache, XIV, 1; Batiffol, *Primitive Catholicism*, p. 105.

would scarcely find much grounds in this text to prove the existence of an obligation requiring the reception of Communion on Sundays. Whereas in the ninth chapter [29] a more solid basis for such a theory might be discovered. The writer gives a description of the Eucharist in which those alone must be allowed to share "who have been baptized into the name of Jesus." Those who suppose the existence of a law making Communion obligatory on Sundays, argue that the Didache here inculcates a precept because it implies that all the faithful had to receive the Eucharist by remarking that the unbaptized must be excluded from the Sacrament. However, the exclusion of the unbaptized was a common custom during the *disciplina arcani,* and does not warrant by any means the assumption that those remaining were bound by precept to receive Communion. Suarez, in treating this question, rejects the existence of a law obliging the weekly reception of the Eucharist in rather summary fashion.[30] Gasparri [31] is also disinclined to accept such a theory, because, granting that the faithful assisting at Mass on Sundays communicated in the first years of the Church, still there is no evidence of a real moral obligation to that effect. Consequently, until further and more solid evidence comes to light, the existence of a precept making the Sunday Communion obligatory, must for the present remain a matter of conjecture.

§ 4. *The Decline of Frequent Communion*

It is very difficult, perhaps impossible, to determine when the old discipline relaxed, and Christians began to communicate but seldom. Until a comparatively late period the fervour of the faithful had dispensed with the necessity of any legislation on the reception of the Eucharist. However, when this pristine fervour had dissipated, it became necessary to formulate precepts for the recep-

[29] Didache, IX, 5.

[30] "Postea creditur determinatio facta ad singulos dies dominicos, de quo etiam non invenio sufficientem traditionem, neque expressum decretum alicujus Pontificis, vel Concilii."—*Opera Omnia,* XXI, q. LXXX, a. XI, disp. LXX, sect. 2.

[31] *Tractatus Canonicus de SS. Eucharistia,* II, 377.

tion of Communion.[32] It does not pertain to this study to inquire into the causes of this falling-off in devotion, whether it proceeded from a general decay of Christian piety, or from a want of strict discipline in the Church, or from a false sense of scrupulosity. But it is true that with the fourth century begin the complaints of the fathers and councils about the negligence of the faithful in receiving Communion. No longer did all the people present at Mass partake of the Body anad Blood of Our Lord. Many approached it only on solemn festivals, some but once a year. As a rule, this laxity was more common in the east than in the west.

The fathers inveighed against this new practice in their writings and in their sermons. But none is more express in this matter, nor more vehement against the neglect of frequent Communion than St. John Chrysostom when he was bishop of Constantinople. "In vain," he bitterly complains, "is the daily Sacrifice, in vain do we stand before the altar, and there is none to partake."[33] In the west the author of the work *De Sacramentis* bears witness to the decline of frequent Communion. It is immaterial here whether St. Ambrose actually wrote or merely inspired this treatise which bears his name, for, regardless of the authorship, it bears eloquent testimony to the growing change in the attitude of the faithful towards the reception of the Eucharist. "For if it is daily bread, why do you receive but annually as the Greeks in the east are wont to do. Receive daily what will daily help you. So live that you may be fit to receive daily."[34]

It was only when lukewarmness began to cool the fervour of Christian souls that the Church, conscious of the ever growing peril of indifference to the Eucharist, began to use the most potent weapon she possessed. Realizing that the time for exhortation alone was at an end, various synods began to formulate decrees for the obligatory reception of the Eucharist, and endeavoured to ensure obedience to them by attaching various sanctions, the most common of which was excommunication. This period of conciliar legislation, broadly speaking, began early in the sixth century and reached its

[32] *Catechism of the Council of Trent*, p. II, c. 4, q. 59.
[33] *In Epist. ad. Ephes. Comment.*, Hom. III—*M. P. G.*, LXII, 29.
[34] *De Sacramentis*, V, 4, 25—*M. P. L.*, XVI, 452.

climax in the Fourth Lateran Council which passed the law regulating the obligatory reception of Communion even down to the present day. The term *broadly speaking* is used advisedly, for some legislation on this matter is found prior to the sixth century.

§ 5. *Legislation in the First Five Centuries*

In the opinion of the best critics, the Apostolic Canons are the expression of ecclesiastical discipline in the east about the time of the third century. Several writers, using the defective translation of Dionysius Exiguus, have seen in the tenth canon an absolute precept that all the faithful who should hear Mass, must communicate.[35] Various interpretations have been placed on this canon; one opinion holding that it applies to those of the faithful who refuse to communicate because of contempt or some superstitious motive, while another opinion, which is the more probable,[36] insists that this canon has only reference to those of the faithful, who instead of hearing the entire Mass by remaining in Church until after the Communion, disturb the services at the altar by leaving after the gospel.[37] This interpretation seems to agree best with the text. Consequently, one cannot deduce from the tenth canon the obligation of communicating at every Mass, but only the obligation of hearing the entire Mass, an obligation which perdures to the present time.

Closely allied to the question of the Apostolic Canons is the controversy surrounding the fragment found in the decree of Gratian attributed to Pope Anacletus.[38] Basing his argument on this fragment, Gratian alleges that it was an apostolic precept that all the faithful should communicate under pain of excommunication. How-

[35] "All such of the faithful as come to church and hear the scriptures read, but stay not for the prayers and to communicate in the Communion, let them be excommunicated as the authors of disorder in the Church."—trans. by Bingham, *Christian Antiquities,* V, 355.

[36] Corblet, *Histoire du Sacrement del' Eucharistie,* I, 351.

[37] Corblet, *ibid.;* Bellarminus, *De Controversiis,* lib. VI, c. X, p. 545.

[38] "Peracta consecratione omnes communicent, qui noluerint carere ecclesiasticis liminibus. Sic enim et Apostoli statuerunt, et sancta Romana tenet ecclesia."—C. 10, D. II, *de cons.*

ever such a conclusion is misleading because of two facts. In the first place, the *Decree of Anacletus* is apocryphal,[39] and consequently cannot be adduced as proving the existence of a precept obliging the reception of the Eucharist at every Mass. Secondly, this fragment should be referred to the ninth apostolic canon [40] which has in view, not the faithful, but the clergy. This canon reads: "If any bishop, presbyter, or deacon, or any other of the clergy does not communicate when the oblation is offered; let him show cause why he does not that; if it be a reasonable cause, he may be excused; but if he show no cause let him be excommunicated as giving scandal to the people, and raising suspicion against him that offers."[41] It is evident that this canon does not warrant one to assume the existence of a law requiring the faithful to receive the Eucharist at every Mass they attended.

While on the whole it is true that ecclesiastical legislation was not required in the first five centuries to compel the faithful to approach the altar, still there are some instances of synods excluding those who were careless in this matter from the meetings of the faithful until they had done penance. For example, the Council of Elvira in 306 gives evidence of the decline of the pious zeal of early Christianity in its twenty-first canon, which runs as follows:—"Si quis in civitate positus tres dominicas ad ecclesiam non accesserit, pauco tempore abstineatur, ut correptus videatur."[42] A similar regulation was introduced at the Council of Sardica in 343 by Hosius.[43] The striking similarity between the legislation of an eastern and a western council may very well be due to the fact that Hosius, who introduced the question at Sardica, was bishop of Cordova in Spain. The omission of Communion on three successive Sundays became, as a consequence of this legislation, the maximum of unpunished negligence. Further dereliction in communicating then incurred a penalty which was not strictly speaking excommunication, but rather a temporary exclusion from offering the oblation,

[39] Berardi, *Gratiani Canones Genuini,* I, p. II, cap. II, p. 27.

[40] Berardi, *ibid.;* Bellarminus, *ibid.;* Rosset, *De Eucharistia,* p. 938.

[41] Trans. by Bingham, *Christian Antiquities,* V, 355.

[42] Schmidt, *Die Bussbücher und die Bussdisciplin der Kirche,* p. 417.

[43] Schmidt, *ibid.*

from participation in the divine services, in prayers, and in the sacraments.[44]

In 341, the Council of Antioch prescribed that "all those who come to the church of God and listen to the reading of the sacred scriptures, but do not take part with the people in prayers, or disdain to partake in common of the Lord's Supper, shall be excluded from the Church till they have done penance and shown signs of reform."[45] Two inferences may be drawn from this prescription of the Council of Antioch. First, the *excommunication* evidently indicates that there was already manifesting itself a tendency towards laxity, and secondly, it is to be noted that legislation regarding the reception of the Eucharist did not yet determine any specific time for such reception.

Eighty years after the Council of Antioch, the first Council of Toledo in 420[46] found it necessary to warn the faithful of the dangers attendant on the neglect of receiving Communion. Its admonitions give the impression that those who were negligent in this regard were considered as suspect of heresy, because in no uncertain terms it advises the faithful to avoid those who were guilty of such dereliction of duty.

In the middle of the fifth century, for the first time conciliar legislation determined a specific period during which it was absolutely necessary for Christians to communicate. To put an end to the laxity of the faithful, a synod held in Ireland, over which St. Patrick is reputed to have presided, decided that "a person cannot be considered one of the faithful who does not communicate on the night of Easter."[47] It is not known precisely during which year this synod was convened, but Mansi places it between the years 450-462. Several writers have referred it to a much later period than the time of St. Patrick, but their arguments are all based upon slight grounds and are for the most part conjectural.[48] It is indeed remarkable that the decree of a particular council of the fifth cen-

[44] Schmidt, *ibid.*

[45] *Conc. in Encoeniis,* c. 2—Mansi, II, 1310.

[46] Mansi, VI, 525.

[47] Mansi, VI, 525.

[48] Moran, *Essays on the Early Irish Church,* p. 181.

tury should essentially coincide with the edict of the Fourth Lateran Council. Both agree on Easter as the time for the obligatory reception of the Eucharist: and both add a grave sanction to the precept. Finally, not until the thirteenth century will any other synod be found which prescribes one Communion in the year as the minimum for satisfying the obligation arising from the divine law.

Article III.—The Obligation of Receiving Communion on Major Feasts

§ 1. *The Council of Agde*

During the fourth and fifth centuries there were indications that the faithful were really indisposed to the frequent reception of the Eucharist. More and more the practice of frequent Communion was weakening, so much so that the distressing situation arose of the Church being compelled to command her subjects to approach the altar. From the sixth century to the thirteenth, particular councils found it advisable to legislate expressly on the obligation of receiving the Eucharist because of the constant conflict between the mind of the Church and the wishes of the faithful in this matter. As a matter of expediency, on the one hand, she no longer expected the practice of frequent Communion, but on the other, she did not feel obliged to limit the obligation of the faithful to a solitary Communion in the year. Not for a moment, moreover, did she cease to counsel her subjects to a more frequent participation in the Body and Blood of Christ.

During the next few centuries the legislative activity of particular councils concerning the obligatory reception of the Eucharist was, to a large extent, to be guided by the prescriptions of the Council of Agde held in 506. This synod, held in Agde, a town in Languedoc, was convened through the efforts of St. Caesarius of Arles, who presided over it. In general its canons shed light on the moral condition of the clergy and the laity in southern France at the beginning of the transition from the Graeco-Roman social order to that of the new barbarian conquerors.[49] The most important canon from

[49] Hefele. *Conciliengeschichte*, II, 649.

the point of view of this study was the eighteenth which considers those who do not communicate on the three great feasts of Christmas, Easter, and Pentecost, as apostates.[50] Bingham dislikes intensely the idea of the Church accommodating herself to the current decline in the fervour of the Christians. He writes: "When matters were come to this degeneracy, some councils, instead of reviving the ancient discipline, and quickening men by just censures to frequent Communion, contented themselves to oblige the faithful to receive three times a year, at the three great festivals, Christmas, Easter, and Pentecost, under the penalty of not being reputed Catholic Christians, if they neglected to communicate at those three noted seasons." [51]

Regarding the Council of Agde it must be remembered that it was not an ecumenical council; its legislation on Communion had far reaching effects, it is true, but nevertheless, it was only a particular council, legislating for a limited area, namely, southern France, outside of which its canons had no juridical force whatsoever. Its importance lies in the fact that it laid down the norm which guided other provincial synods for a long time to come; a norm which in the course of time practically became the unwritten law of the universal Church.

Before further tracing the trend of legislation on the reception by precept of Holy Communion, it is necessary to investigate very briefly the reasons for the choice of Christmas, Easter, and Pentecost, as the feasts on which Christians were obliged to communicate. The selection of Easter causes no particular difficulty. The greatest festival of the year is undoubtedly that of Our Lord's Resurrection, and as such it has ever been selected, either in union with other days, or in preference to them, as the proper time for receiving the Eucharist.[52] The season in which the Eucharist itself was instituted seems always to have been, in the mind of the Church, the time most fitting for the reception of Him Who made it possible. Hence, even during the lifetime of St. John Chrysostom, the reception of the Eucharist was so allied to the feast of the Resurrection

[50] Mansi, VIII, 327.

[51] *Christian Antiquities,* V, 371.

[52] Bridgett, *A History of the Holy Eucharist in Great Britain,* II, 257.

that the phrase "to make one's Easter duty" was synonymous with communicating.[53] In the middle ages this was so much the case that the characteristic feature of this festival was the general Communion of the people.[54] Christmas and Pentecost, the other two feasts, have not the same traditions as Easter as proper periods for receiving the Eucharist, but nevertheless it was always considered peculiarly fitting that the faithful should communicate on these two feasts which commemorate the principal mysteries of religion.[55]

It has already been noted that the Council of Agde, which first prescribed three Communions of obligation in the year, did not legislate for the entire Church. Consequently those parts of the Church which did not come under its influence, in many instances differed in their practice regarding the reception of Communion. But the fact that so many provincial councils did adopt the decree of Agde, in the spirit if not in the letter, argues well not only for the expediency but also the necessity of a precept allowing a minimum of observance in the matter. It was expedient because it ensured a periodic approach to the Sacrament which otherwise might have been entirely neglected; and it was necessary because to require more might mean numerous sins of omission on the part of the faithful.

It will not be necessary in the following section to give a complete catalogue of all the synods and episcopal constitutions which adopted the prescription of the Languedoc council, for the general trend of legislation will be sufficiently indicated by the citation of those which are outstanding.

§ 2. *From Agde to Gratian*

In another part of France an important council was held at Autun in 670 for the purpose of regulating the discipline of the Benedictine monasteries. However, so grave a problem had been caused by the alarming falling off in the reception of Holy Communion that this council interrupted its other business long enough to repeat substantially the decree of Agde.[56] Egbert, archbishop of

[53] Corblet, *Histoire du Sacrement del'Eucharistie*, I, 353.

[54] Probst, *Sakramente und Sakramentalien*, p. 236.

[55] Benedict XIV, *De Synodo Dioecesana*, lib. V, cap. I, n. 7.

[56] *Conc. Augustodunen.*, c. 14—Mansi, XI, 126.

York, 732-766, a strict disciplinarian, thought fit to introduce the same prescription in northern England, for among the extracts known as the *Excerptiones e dictis et canonibus ss. patrum*[57] is found the law making the reception of Communion obligatory three times in the year.[58] The introduction of this legislation by Egbert was opportune, because, although it was scarce a hundred years since the conversion of Northumbria by St. Aidan and St. Oswald, fervour had so cooled that the practice of frequent Communion among seculars was practically unknown in that part of England.[59]

In the early part of the ninth century the laity are again commanded to communicate at least three times a year by the third Council of Tours.[60] Two points in this canon are worthy of comment. First, the Council did not define on which feasts the reception of the Eucharist was obligatory. As a rule, very few disciplinary canons during this period fail to do so. Secondly, the phrase *etsi non frequentius* is indicative of an attitude which the Church has never relinquished. In her prudence, she is ever loath to place a too stringent obligation on the faithful, but at the same time she never fails to exhort her children to the more frequent approach to the fount of all grace.

The prescription of the Council of Agde was reaffirmed, not only by the canons of various diocesan and provincial synods, but also by divers collections of capitularies. The capitularies or *capitula* of the bishops were compilations of ecclesiastical laws, drawn as a rule from previous legislation, and proposed to the clergy and people for their guidance. Their general purpose, on the one hand, was to make it easy for ecclesiastics to have an intimate knowledge of the laws of the Church; on the other, to keep intact and uniform her discipline, and to maintain the religious life of both clergy and laity at as high a standard as possible.

About the middle of the ninth century, Jonas, bishop of Orleans,

[57] Mansi, XII, 411-432.

[58] Mansi, XII, 417.

[59] Bridgett, *op. cit.*, I, 220.

[60] The canon in question reads: "If not more frequently, lay people must communicate three times in the year, unless prevented perchance by some of the greater sins."—*Conc. Turon.*, c. 50—Mansi, XIV, 91.

who played an important rôle in the ecclesiastical affairs of France, deplores the fact that the greater part of the faithful absent themselves from Communion except on the occasion of the three great festivals, Christmas, Pentecost, and Easter, when they approach the Sacrament more from habit than devotion.[61] An interesting deduction may be drawn from this work, namely, that the faithful were already limiting themselves to the three Communions in the year from habit, and this habit, no doubt, was based upon their realization of the obligation to approach the altar at least three times a year.

Towards the end of the ninth century, Vulfrade, bishop of Bourges, in a pastoral letter to his priests and people, demands that the faithful, excepting only public sinners, should communicate worthily at Christmas, Easter, and Pentecost.[62]

The two works already quoted were not strictly speaking capitularies. However, the following capitularies indicate that the obligation to communicate on the three major feasts was slowly becoming the universal policy of the Church. The eighteenth canon of the synod of Agde was reproduced in identical terms by Atto of Verceil, who lived from 924-961 [63]; Regino of Prum [64]; Burchard [65]; the divers collections of the capitularies of Ansegise; [66] and finally, by Yves of Chartres.[67]

In the beginning of the eleventh century, at a time when the Danes were overrunning England, a council held at Aenham exhorted the people to have recourse to penance and the Eucharist. "Let every Christian, as the most necessary exercise of his faith and Christian profession frequently go to his confessor. . . . Let him also reverently prepare to receive the Holy Eucharist as often as it may seem necessary to him, *but at least three times a year.*" [68]

[61] *De Institutione laicali,* lib. II, c. XVIII—*M. P. L.*, CVI, 202; Dublanchy, "Communion Eucharistique," *Dict. de Théol. Cath.*, III, 522.

[62] *Epis. Pastor. ad parochos et parochianos suos*—*M. P. L.*, CXXI, 1140.

[63] *Capit.*, c. LXIII—Mansi, XIX, 257.

[64] *De Eccles. Disciplin.*, lib. II, c. V—*M. P. L.*, CXXXII, 285.

[65] *Decret.*, lib. V, c. XVII—*M. P. L.*, CXL, 756.

[66] *Capitul. Ansegis.*, lib. II, c. XLV—*M. P. L.*, XCVII, 547.

[67] *Decret.*, p. II, c. XXVII—*M. P. L.*, CLXL, 167.

[68] *Conc. Aenhamen.* c. XX—Mansi, XIX, 308-309.

§ 3. *The Decree of Gratian*

The precept obliging the reception of Communion three times a year was incorporated in the Decree of Gratian[69] which was written about 1142, and now for the first time the ordinance of the Council of Agde assumed the character of a general law. In two different canons, the sixteenth and the nineteenth, Gratian mentions the obligation of receiving Communion three times a year, even specifying the particular feasts on which this duty was to be fulfilled. Many writers have discussed Gratian's crediting Pope Fabian with this legislation. On the one hand, Van Espen,[70] Devoti,[71] Ferraris [72] and Corblet,[73] all take him to task for referring it back to Fabian. On the other, Benedict XIV[74] does not take exception to the reference, but follows Burchard[75] without question. There seems to be a real discrepancy in Gratian. Ferraris and Van Espen argue that in the time of Fabian it is certain that the Christians communicated very frequently, and for that reason, it would have been wholly illogical for the Pope to pass a law requiring the reception of the Eucharist three times a year. Such a law would not have been reasonable in an epoch during which the faithful were still imbued with apostolic zeal and fervour, and besides it is singular that the Popes, during the five succeeding centuries, did not renew a prescription which was then made because of the relaxation of the laity. But there still remains the problem of Burchard and Gratian. Berardi[76] gives the solution. The fragment cannot be credited to Fabian, but more properly it is an excerpt from the capitularies of the French kings. Burchard probably was cognizant of this fact, but he did not dare arouse the indignation of the Germans for whom he was writing, by giving the true origin of the law. Consequently he attributed it to Fabian, and Gratian accepted the reference with-

[69] C. 16, 19, D. II, *de cons.*

[70] *Opera Omnia,* p. II, sect. I, tit. IV, *de Sac. Eucharistiae,* c. III, 3.

[71] *Institutionum Canonicarum Libri IV*—II, 86.

[72] *Bibliotheca,* v. *Eucharistia,* III, n. 111.

[73] *Histoire du Sacrement del' Eucharistie,* I, 352.

[74] *De Synodo Dioecesana,* lib. V, cap. I, n. 7.

[75] *Decret.,* lib. V, c. XVII—*M. P. L.,* CXL, 756.

[76] *Gratiani Canones Genuini,* I, p. II, cap. XVIII, p. 108.

out criticism. This solution seems to give an adequate explanation of the whole problem.

§4. *Stricter Obligations*

It would be a grave mistake to conclude that the Church everywhere was satisfied with prescribing three Communions of obligation in the year. The obligation demanded by the Council of Agde was the minimum required by the law. Ordinarily to comply with its letter was not held to be satisfactory, and consequently, the bishops tried every means in their power to obtain more. In some places hope had not yet been giving up of persuading the faithful to approach the altar every Sunday. For example, in France only eighty years after the Council of Agde, a council held under St. Ammacharius at Auxerre urged weekly Communion.[77] A like effort was made by a Bavarian council which appeals to the practice of weekly Communion among the Greeks and the Romans.[78] Attempts at reform were not confined to France and Germany. The *Penitentiale Casinense* which was written about the end of the ninth century, is representative of the discipline in Italy. This penitential code declares that all Christians should communicate every Sunday as is the wont of the Greeks.[79]

The penitential codes are of great assistance in determining the ecclesiastical discipline of the Church during the Middle Ages. It is only within the last fifty years that writers on this question have begun to appreciate the influence exercised by the penitential of St. Cummian in the formation of the disciplinary code in England and western Europe. No fewer than six penitentials, based upon the penitential code of this saint, and compiled before the tenth century, are given by Wasserschleben. The custom with regard to the reception of the Eucharist is found in one of the canons of St. Cummian's Penitential. "Greci omni dominica communicant, clerici et laici,

[77] Mansi, IX, 911; cf. Mourou, "Communion Eucharistique," *Dict. de Théol. Cath.*, 484.

[78] *Conc. Bajuwaric.* (740), c. VI—*Mon. Germ. Hist., Concilia,* II, 52.

[79] *Poenitentiale Casinense,* c. 91—Schmidt, *Die Bussbücher und die Bussdisciplin der Kirche,* p. 417; Dublanchy, "Communion Eucharistique," *Dict. de Théol. Cath.*, 526.

et qui in tribus dominicis non communicaverint excommunicentur, sicut canones habent. Romani similiter communicant, qui volunt, qui autem noluerint, non excommunicantur."[80] This canon defined sharply the difference in the eucharistic discipline of the Greek and Latin churches. Weekly Communion was a matter of obligation for the Greeks, the neglect of which over a period of three Sundays carried with it an excommunication. On the contrary, weekly reception of the Eucharist was a matter of counsel for the Roman church.

St. Theodore of Canterbury has long been famed as the great founder of the penitential code of the western Church during the eighth and succeeding centuries. Yet few care to call attention to the fact that St. Cummian's work was the basis of Theodore's penitential, and that many of the decrees referred to the great archbishop of Canterbury were adopted verbatim from Cummian.[81] Consequently it is not surprising to find in Theodore's Penitential the canon quoted above, with but a slight change in order.[82]

In spite of all invitations and admonitions, frequent Communion did not strike root among the greater number of the laity. In the very country where Theodore of Canterbury was labouring to introduce it, the Council of Cloveshow gave up all hope of success, and seeing that many sorely lacked the necessary dispositions, turned to the children and the aged, and asked that at least the young children in whom the passions were still dormant, and the old people who had ceased to sin, be exhorted to receive the Eucharist more frequently.[83]

A more significant event occurred in the conversion of the Bulgarians about the year 860. More savage neophytes never entered the Church, yet Pope Nicholas earnestly exhorted them to communicate daily during Lent.[84]

Besides the three Communions prescribed by the Council of Agde and succeeding councils, it became customary to approach the altar

[80] XIV, 4—Schmidt, *op. cit.*, p. 644.

[81] Moran, *Essays on the Origin, Doctrines, and Discipline of the Early Irish Church*, p. 255.

[82] Th. I, 12, §1, 2.—Schmidt, *op. cit.*, p. 534.

[83] *Conc. Cloveshov.* II (747), c. XXIII—Mansi, XII, 402.

[84] *M. P. L.*, CXIX, 983, 984; cf. Villien, *A History of the Commandments*, p. 198.

on the day of the institution of the Eucharist, Holy Thursday. Every Christian was bound to communicate at Easter, Pentecost, and Christmas, but according to Ratherius of Verona [85] the Easter Communion was twofold; one Communion was to be received on Holy Thursday, the other on Easter Sunday. This custom soon became a strict obligation, because according to the Decree of Burchard [86] the omission of any of the four Communions was a sin to be confessed.

§5. *Further Relaxation in Communicating*

The precept of Agde, provincial in origin, had gradually extended its sphere of influence beyond the limits of France. Its wholehearted adoption in so many places had given it a note of universality which properly did not belong to it. Yet in the course of time the precept ordering the faithful to communicate three times a year took on the form of exhortation rather than of obligation, with the result that in many places precept resolved itself into mere counsel. It is almost impossible to determine when this transition was effected.[87] The fact that this change took place at a time when the Church was entering the golden period of her power has puzzled many writers. It is not within the purview of this study to trace the various causes of such a paradox, but in general it may be said that the invasions of the Normans, the Saracens, and the Magyars interrupted to a great degree the orderly routine of ecclesiastical discipline.[88] When order finally was restored, it was found impossible to enforce the former discipline.[89] As a consequence, by the

[85] *Epist. Synodica ad Presbyteros,* n. 10—*M. P. L.*, CXXXVI, 562.

[86] Lib. XXX, c. V—*M. P. L.*, CXL, 963.

[87] Van Espen, *Jus Ecclesiasticum Universum,* II, sect. I, t. IV, *de sac. eucharistiae,* c. III, n. 4.

[88] In this connection the following excerpt is apropos: ". . . when every coast was ravaged by pagan Normans, and no inland city on a river's bank was safe; when the Saracens had the possession of the Mediterranean, and savage hordes of wild Magyars overran northern Italy and Germany, the tremendous physical suffering inflicted on Christendom left the faithful but little time for devotion."—Dalgairns, *The Holy Communion,* p. 220.

[89] As Corblet so aptly puts it, there had taken place "un grand refroidissement dans les pratiques de la piété."—*Histoire du Sacrement del' Eucharistie,* I, 353.

tacit permission of the Church[90] the obligation of communicating had been reduced to the solemnity of Easter, and this was, towards the end of the middle ages, the lone Communion of the year for the majority of the people.[91] This was the prevailing condition in the Church at the beginning of the thirteenth century, sometimes called the greatest of centuries. It was truly an alarming condition, and one calling for an immediate remedy. This remedy was forthcoming in the legislation of the Fourth Lateran Council.

Article IV.—The Decree of the Fourth Lateran Council

§1. *The Fourth Lateran Council*

The culminating point of the mediaeval splendour of the Church is the Fourth Lateran Council. Not at Nicaea itself was there a more august representation of the Christian world.[92] Yet it was precisely then, when the world was at her feet, that the Church was compelled to enact penalties against her children who did not communicate once a year, and to limit her commands to an Easter Communion because she did not dare require more. This famous council was convened by Pope Innocent III. He was not only for his time an energetic reformer of ecclesiastical discipline and the world dominating ruler of Christianity, but for all time he has erected a monument to his far seeing pastoral solicitude in the famous decree on Easter Communion. For under his direction and determining influence the general council drew up that memorable resolution which even in its verbal form has not yet disappeared from ecclesiastical legislation. The timeliness of this decree has been pointed out by Leo XIII.[93] "And indeed," writes the Pontiff, "it was a needful measure of precaution against a complete falling away that Innocent III, in the Council of the Lateran, most strictly enjoined that no Christian should abstain from receiving the Communion of the Lord's Body at least in the Paschal season." Another reason must not be

[90] Benedict XIV, *De Synodo Dioecesana*, lib. V, c. I, n. 7.

[91] Baumgärtler, *Die Erstkommunion der Kinder*, p. 207.

[92] Dalgairns, *The Holy Communion*, p. 221.

[93] Litt. Encycl. "*Mirae Çaritatis*," 28 maii 1902.—*Fontes*, n. 648.

overlooked in determining the action of the Fathers in their selection of Easter as the season for the satisfaction of the divino-ecclesiastical obligation of receiving the Eucharist. A perusal of the last article will call attention to the lack of uniformity in regard to the Communion of precept. Prior to 1215, efforts to correct this difference in custom were never entirely satisfactory due to the fact that whatever conciliar action was undertaken had been provincial, and hence limited in scope. A universal law was required to bring about that unity of discipline so necessary for a Church possessing the note of unity. This the Fourth Lateran Council accomplished by requiring nothing more than the minimum universally required.[94] Its action resulted in the promulgation of a general law binding the whole Church, for it was an ecumenical council, and as such, its legislation affected the whole body of the faithful. The prescriptions concerning Confession and the annual Communion were joined in the famous twenty-first canon, which reads:

> Omnis utriusque sexus fidelis, postquam ad annos discretionis pervenerit, omnia sua solus peccata saltem semel in anno fideliter confiteatur proprio sacerdoti, et injunctam sibi poenitentiam sibi pro viribus studeat adimplere, suscipiens reverenter ad minus in Pascha Eucharistiae sacramentum, nisi forte de consilio proprii sacerdotis ob aliquam rationabilem causam ad tempus ab ejus perceptione duxerit abstinendum; alioquin et vivens ab ingressu ecclesiae arceatur et moriens christiana careat sepultura. Unde hoc salutare statutum frequenter in ecclesiis publicetur, ne quisquam ignorantiae caecitate velamen excusationis assumat. . . . [95]

Few disciplinary canons have obtained a success equal to this one. After seven hundred years it still remains substantially unchanged through all the varied vicissitudes of the Church, for the Easter Communion as laid down by the Lateran Council differs but little from that prescribed by the Code. No startling innovation was made when this famous decree was drawn up. The custom of receiving Communion at Easter was as old as the Church herself; but the fact that this customary reception of the Eucharist at Easter was made the sole Communion of precept for the entire Church, was something new.

[94] Cf. Villien, *A History of the Commandments*, p. 204.

[95] *Conc. Lateranense IV*—Mansi, XXII, 1007.

An analysis of the decree brings to light the following points. The obligations imposed are: First, every Christian of either sex who has attained the use of reason must receive the Eucharist at Easter. Secondly, he or she can be exempted by the pastor only by way of exception and for reasonable motives. Finally, disobedience is punishable by a double penalty, exclusion from the Church during life, and privation of Christian burial after death. It should be noted also that the obligation binding the faithful is twofold: first, they are obliged to communicate once a year, and secondly, they are bound to satisfy this obligation during the paschal season. It is evident that the former obligation is the principal one, being, as it were, the determination of Christ's command to partake of His Body and Blood, and consequently a graver obligation than the latter which is purely ecclesiastical in origin.[96]

Durandus is the only theologian, who, by means of minute subtleties, has raised the doubt whether the constitution of the Lateran Council enacts a true precept or simply gives utterance to an exhortation.[97] He implies this by vague innuendoes rather than by a positive statement, but he does not dare deny that the Church has the power to oblige the faithful to frequent the Sacraments.[98]

Several important questions arise in a detailed discussion of the decree, such as the length of the paschal season, the determination of the ecclesiastical year, the rite of the precept, but since they are still points of importance in the present legislation, they will be treated in detail in the commentary on the canons under which they fall. The purpose of the present historical synopsis is merely to trace the evolution of the law itself and to consider those questions of historical import which are not found in the Code today.

§2. *The Effects of the Clause "Ad Minus"*

The Lateran decree had created a new legislation, but it did not make this new legislation irreconcilable with the old, nor did it

[96] Gasparri, *De SS. Eucharistia*, n. 1157; Mourou, "Communion Eucharistique," *Dict. de Théol. Cath.*, I, 485; Villien, *op. cit.*, p. 204.

[97] Corblet, *Histoire du Sacrement del' Eucharistie*, I, 354.

[98] "De la Confessione Annuelle et de la Communion Pascale," *Analecta Juris Pontificii* (1860), c. 2265.

abrogate the provincial and synodal statutes which obliged the faithful to communicate more than once a year. The diocesan laws remained in force and as obligatory as before; to disobey them exposed one to the existing diocesan penalties.[99] Legislation requiring more than one Communion in the year seemed nothing else than an interpretation of the words *ad minus* in the decree. The Easter Communion was, as it were, the minimum conceded to negligent Christians, the final limit of tolerance, the omission of which raised the suspicion of heresy against the offender. But the addition of the words *ad minus* indicates that the Church was not content with a solitary Communion in the year. This is the reason why a certain number of provincial councils, sensing this attitude of the Fathers of the Lateran, continued to prescribe the reception of the Eucharist on the three great festivals, as heretofore, during the thirteenth and fourteenth centuries.[100] It will suffice at this point to cite a few instances of such legislation.

In the Constitutions of Richard of Sarum,[101] the following prescription is found. "Communion must be received three times, at Easter, Pentecost, and Christmas . . . whosoever does not receive the sacrament of the Eucharist once a year . . . at least at Easter time, unless he abstain on the advice of his pastor, must be prevented from entering the Church during life, and after death must be deprived of Christian burial." An identical decree is found in the constitutions of St. Edmund of Canterbury.[102]

At Toulouse it seems that the diocesan authorities tried to establish a singularly severe discipline for which the Lateran decree was to serve as a basis. A decree resembling it in tenor obliged all Christians to go to Confession and Communion three times in the year under pain of being suspect of heresy.[103] This particular discipline was so carefully couched in the phraseology of the general de-

[99] Villien, *op. cit.*, p. 206.

[100] Corblet, *op. cit.*, I, 354.

[101] *Constit. Ricardi* (1217), c. XXV—Mansi, XXII, 1115; Harduin, VII, 96.

[102] *Const. S. Edmundi Cantuar.*, c. XVIII—Mansi, XXIII, 421; Harduin, VII, 270.

[103] *Conc. Toles.*—Mansi, XXIII, 197; Harduin, VII, 178.

cree that the inattentive reader might imagine, in reading it, that he had before him the Lateran canon.[104]

To maintain this twofold discipline as laid down by the general law of the Church, on one hand, and by the decrees of the provincial synods on the other, became more and more difficult. Very soon the sanctions attached to the non-fulfillment of the particular laws vanished, and after that, it was only a question of time until the Communion required by the Fourth Lateran Council became the sole obligatory one in the year. From the first half of the thirteenth century, some statutes admit only the Easter Communion as of precept,[105] and little by little, the constitutions of the diocesan synods mention none other. As a result, the obligation of receiving Communion three times a year, first promulgated by the Council of Agde, soon ceased to have any juridical force whatsoever. The Council of Toledo, it is true, mentions the three Communions in the year, but it does this to call attention to the fact that the clergy should frequent the Sacrament of the Eucharist more often than the laity.[106]

§3. *Promulgation of the Lateran Decree*

Few disciplinary canons have attained the success of the Lateran decree. This seems to have been due to the wise forethought of the legislators when they inserted the following words in the body of the text: "Unde hoc salutare statutum frequenter in ecclesiis publicetur, ne quisquam ignorantiae caecitate velamen excusationis assumat." Even today the Roman Ritual[107] requires that pastors see to it that the faithful be reminded of their Easter duty sometime during Lent. This is the general law today, but for some time

[104] The provincial Council of Albi in 1254 also insisted on the obligation of communicating three times in the year. (*Conc. Albiens.*, c. XXI—Mansi, XXIII, 840; Harduin, VII, 462.) The same legislation is found in the decrees of the provincial Council of Treves held in 1310. (*Conc. Trevirens.*—Mansi, XXV, 286.)

[105] *Conc. Cenomanen.* (*Le Mans*), (1247)—Mansi, XXIII, 746; *Conc. Claromontana* (1268)—Mansi, XXIII, 1192.

[106] "Alii vero clerici, ut ostendant se ad plus teneri quam laici, ad minus communicent ter in anno."—*Conc. Toletan.* (1324), c. VII—Mansi, XXV, 734.

[107] Tit. IV, cap. III, n. 1.

after the Lateran Council, the promulgation of the law varied as much as had the practice of receiving the Eucharist in the first centuries of the Church's existence. Several councils [108] ordered that the decree be published at the beginning of Lent. But such promulgation was not always sufficient to produce the desired result, for which reason councils held at Tarragona [109] and Salamanca [110] required that the precept be published four times in the year. So important did several councils consider this aspect of the Lateran decree that they did not hesitate to punish negligence on the part of pastor in publishing it. For example the Council of Bourges [111] ordered the pastors, under pain of excommunication, to procure for themselves a copy of the decree in both Latin and the vernacular so that they might be able to give the best possible explanation to the laity. The Council of Ravenna [112] was not content with the publication of the decree during Lent, but required that the clergy, the pastors in particular, should speak of it in their sermons during Advent. Another council, which was held at Valladolid in 1327, shows the greatest solicitude for the promulgation of the Lateran canon, because it orders that it be published, under pain of excommunication, on every Sunday from Septuagesima to Easter.[113]

During the next few centuries many synods remind the clergy of their duty in bringing the Lateran decree to the attention of the faithful. No new methods of promulgating the decree are mentioned, and consequently it will suffice to mention just a few; for example, Augsburg [114] held by Cardinal Othon in 1548 insists on the promulgation of the Lateran legislation, as does the provincial

[108] *Rouen.* (1223)—Harduin, VII, 128; *Conc. Claromontan.* (1268)—Mansi, XXIII, 1192; Harduin, VII, 594; *Sens.* (1269), c. IV—Mansi, XXIV, 5; Harduin, VII, 650; *Trèves* (1277), c. V—Mansi, XXIV, 192; *Pont-Audemer* (1279), c. V—Mansi, XXIV, 222; *Nimes,* c. XIII—Mansi, XXIV, 631; *Coutances* (1300), c. XXXIII—Mansi, XXV, 37-38.

[109] *Conc. Terraconen.* (1329), c. LXCII—Mansi, XXV, 870.

[110] *Conc. Salmanticen.* (1335), c. XVI, n. 41—Mansi, XXV, 1057.

[111] (1286)—Harduin, VII, 954.

[112] (1311)—Harduin, VII, 1367.

[113] Mansi, XXV, 722.

[114] Harduin, IX, 2041.

Council of Mexico in 1585,[115] the Council of Avignon in 1594 [116], and the Council of Bordeaux in 1624.[117] One of the principal reasons why so much stress was laid upon this particular point of the decree was the sanction attached to the neglect of the paschal precept. Ignorance would excuse from the penalty, and since the Lateran council hoped to ensure the fulfilling of the precept by means of the sanction, it insisted on the publication of the whole decree very strongly so that no one could feign ignorance.

§4. *The Age of Discretion*

As far back as the third century evidence shows that it was not uncommon for infants to receive Communion immediately after they were baptized.[118] They communicated under the species of wine when they were very young, and under the species of bread when capable. This practice of administering Holy Communion to children who had not yet attained the use of reason continued in use throughout the whole Church till the twelfth century. In the East the custom was almost universal and is still prevalent in some places, but in the West it almost disappeared about the ninth century because of the dangers of profanation, irreverence, and other inconveniences.[119] It was left to the Fourth Lateran Council to determine the status of children as subjects of Communion. It supposes the general prevalence of the contrary custom, and indirectly gives it its sanction when in the decree on annual Communion it declares it obligatory only after one reaches the age of discretion.[120]

[115] Harduin, X, 1659.

[116] Harduin, X, 1846.

[117] Harduin, XI, 70.

[118] St. Cyprian, "*De Lapsis,*" XXV—*M. P. L.*, IV, 484. Cf. S. C. C. "*Quam Singulari,*" 8 Aug., 1910—*A. A. S.*, II (1910), 577.

[119] Such reasons prompted the third Council of Tours to forbid priests to administer the Eucharist to young children—*Conc. Turonen.* (813), c. XIX—Mansi, XIV, 89.

[120] Johann Ernst, in his article "*Die Zeit der ersten hl. kommunion und die Jahre der Unterderscheidung seit dem IV. allgem. Konzil vom Lateran*" (AkKR, CVII, 433-497, 1927) denies the contention, in opposition to the general interpretation of canonists, that the Lateran Council required the age of reason as a necessary condition of admission to Holy Communion.

Granting that the Lateran Council did not expressly prohibit the custom of infant Communion, yet it is noteworthy that from this time on it became customary *not* to admit children to the Sacrament of the Eucharist until the dawn of reason.[121] For example, two councils during the thirteenth century prohibited the administration of this sacrament to children under the age of seven years.[122] The Council of Trent reiterated and confirmed the decree of the Lateran Council,[123] although it did not condemn the ancient discipline of giving Holy Communion to children before they had attained the use of reason.[124] However, under pain of anathema, it declared that the Eucharist is not necessary for salvation in the case of little children before they arrive at the age of discretion.[125]

The comparatively recent legislation on the reception of the Eucharist constitutes a new era in the history of this sacrament. To one class of persons the Church looks for the most valuable results as the outcome of this legislation, namely, to the young. The decree "Quam Singulari" corrected the abuses which tended to delay the admission of children to Holy Communion to an age which was contrary to the spirit of the decree of the Lateran Council. The rigorous spirit which characterised the requirements for the reception of the Eucharist by children before the timely legislation of Pius X, was in large part due to the disastrous influence of Jansenism. The deferring of the approach to the altar to an age as late as fourteen was one of the most unfortunate results of this insidious heresy. It seems incredible that such a practice could have developed in the face of the seemingly clear expression "age of discretion" *(annos discretionis)* of the Lateran decree.

The Lateran Council had declared that every faithful Catholic was held to confess and communicate when he had attained discretionary powers. On analysis, this formula which *prima facie* would

[121] Many, *Praelectiones de Missa,* p. 299.

[122] *Council of Rouen* (1235), c. XIX—Mansi, XXIII, 376; *Council of Bayeux* (1300)—Mansi, XXV, 63.

[123] *Conc. Trid.,* Sess. XIII, *de Eucharistia,* c. IX—Mansi, XXIII, 85; Waterworth, *Canons and Decrees of the Council of Trent,* p. 83.

[124] *Conc. Trid.,* Sess. XXI, *de Communione,* cap. 4—Mansi, XXIII, 123; Waterworth, *op. cit.,* p. 142.

[125] *Ibid.*

seem to offer no difficulty, is susceptible of different interpretations. The decree did not state at what age a child attained the age of discretion. For this reason some particular councils took upon themselves the task of supplying this want.[126]

This diversity in explaining the Lateran canon would be surprising if the cause were not known. If the councils of the thirteenth century delayed the obligation of annual Communion to the age of twelve and fourteen, it was not because the children of that time were less developed than those of modern times, but because the authorities wished to delay the obligation imposed by the law until puberty.[127] To use scholastic terminology, the obligations imposed by the canon were taken not *in sensu diviso* but *in sensu composito*. The canon was considered as comprising, not various obligations, but one obligation which included both the precept of Communion and Confession, besides the penalties threatened by both. Because of this interpretation, the age was placed much higher than the Council ever intended it to be. Since penalties of the positive law did not affect those who had not reached the age of puberty, it followed that children were not bound by this composite obligation until they were twelve or fourteen years of age.[128] Later on, it was taught that the precept was to be taken *in sensu diviso* and that therefore the canon *"Omnis utriusque"* obliged all who had attained the age of discretion. In the case of children, the penalties were only incurred when the age of puberty was reached.[129] That the Council of Trent evidently understood the Lateran expression *annos discretionis* as signifying the use of reason, may be gathered from an analysis of the legislation on Communion.[130] For the two expressions *"parvuli usu rationis carentes"* and *"parvuli antequam ad annos discretionis pervenerunt"*

[126] *Conc. Narbonen.* (1227), c. VII—Mansi, XXIII, 23; *Synod. Lucana* (1308), c. LVII—Mansi, XXV, 189; *Conc. Biterren.* (1351), c. XII—Mansi, XXVI, 250. These councils give a determined age, namely, fourteen years. At Tarragona a distinction between boys and girls was established as to when the age of obligation began, fourteen for the former, and twelve for the latter.—*Conc. Terraconen.* (1329), c. LXVII—Mansi, XXVI, 870.

[127] Villien, *A History of the Commandments of the Church*, p. 172.

[128] De Lugo, *de Eucharistia*, disp. XIII, sect. IV, n. 33.

[129] Villien, *op. cit.*, p. 174.

[130] *Conc. Trident.*, Sess. XXI, cap. IV, can. IV.

are used indiscriminately for one another, giving the impression that the Council considered them as synonymous.[131] This but confirms the opinion which maintains that the Lateran Council understood the term "age of discretion" as equivalent to the use of reason.

§5. *The Penalties*

The third part of the decree determined the penalties for disobedience, namely, exclusion from church during life and after death. In other words dereliction in the fulfillment of the Easter duty brought with it the double penalty of exclusion from participation in ecclesiastical services during life, or personal interdict, and refusal of Christian burial after death. The use of the word *arceatur* indicates that the former penalty was *ferendae sententiae;* on the contrary the word *careat* signifies that the latter penalty was *latae sententiae.*[132] All the councils and synods which followed the Lateran, faithfully renewed this sanction. Moreover, the penalties affected not only those who violated both precepts, of annual Confession and Easter Communion, but also those who violated either one of the two.[133] These penalties were not incurred before the legal age of puberty. Nor could they be enforced except in cases where the delinquents were known. For this reason, synodal and provincial statutes directed the pastors to keep a roster of all persons subject to the precept. Such, for example, is the ruling of a council held at Toledo.[134]

For some time the exclusion from church of those who had not made their Easter duty at the appointed time was observed with great strictness, for theologians held all those who passed more than a year without recourse to the Eucharist as suspect of heresy.[135] But in proportion as the number of the guilty increased, the application of the penalty became necessarily less rigorous; if the persons who frequented church fulfilled their other duties, they were not to be

[131] Gasparri, *De SS. Eucharistia,* n. 1167.

[132] Gasparri, *op. cit.,* n. 1172.

[133] *Conc. Narbonen.* (1227), c. VII—Mansi, XXIII, 23.

[134] *Conc. Toletan.* (1339), c. V—Mansi, XXV, 1146.

[135] Fagnani, *Jus Canonicum, sive Commentarium in Decretales,* in c. *Omnis, De Poenitent. et Remissionibus,* n. 15.

expelled if they stayed away from the altar through negligence or human respect.

The Council of Trent [136] placed an excommunication on all those who have denied that all Christians are bound by this precept, which censure, since it was enacted directly by the Fathers, remained after the constitution *"Apostolicae Sedis"* [137] in which it does not obtain mention. The force of this censure lies in the fact that one who habitually omits his Easter Communion, is deservedly suspected of heresy. This, however, is a doctrinal rather than a disciplinary measure. Unfortunately, in spite of all these precautions, the relaxation did not cease. In the latter part of the nineteenth century, the only penalty which was still enforced was the refusal of Christian burial, and even this applied in practice only to those who neglected their Easter duty for many years, and died without giving any signs of contrition. Today, the Code has omitted the ancient sanction from the law, and consequently, it can be no longer taught or preached that a Catholic who omits his Easter duty for one year or for many, is excommunicated and loses his right to Christian burial.

§6. *The Lateran Decree in the Decretals and the Council of Trent*

From the Fourth Lateran Council to the present time, no new general legislation has exacted more than the one Communion in the year. The decree passed into the Decretals of Gregory IX, where it is reiterated in its entirety and without any change whatsoever.[138] The Council of Trent [139] confirmed it without changing it in any detail.

In the United States, the Second Plenary Council of Baltimore, 1866, contains the following decree: "Ne itaque in tanta re officio nostro deesse videamur, decretum illud celebre, quod Patres Concilii Lateranensis IV de annua communione sanxerunt, quodque voluerunt ut 'frequenter in ecclesiis publicaretur, ne quispiam ignorantiae caeci-

[136] Sess. XIII, *de ss. eucharistia,* cap. 8, can. 9.

[137] 12 Oct. 1869—*Fontes,* n. 552; Gasparri, *loc. cit.*

[138] C. 12, X, *de cons.,* V, 38.

[139] Sess. XIII, *de Eucharistia,* can. 9—Mansi, XXXIII, 85.

tate velamen excusationis assumeret' hic rursus ipsis eorundem Patrum verbis promulgamus 'Omnis . . . . sepultura.' "[140] Consequently, this council renewed the Lateran decree without change for the United States, even insisting on the sanction added by the Fathers. As has been said, this penalty can no longer be enforced.

The Lateran legislation passed into the Code, retaining to a large extent its ancient form. The new discipline differs, however, in many points from the old, and these will be treated extensively in the commentary on the canons under which they fall.

[140] *Acta et Decreta Conc. Plenarii Baltimor. II*, n. 255.

CHAPTER III

THE SUBJECT OF THE PRECEPT

Canon 859. § 1. Omnis utriusque sexus fidelis, postquam ad annos discretionis, idest ad usum rationis, pervenerit, debet semel in anno, saltem in Paschate, Eucharistiae sacramentum recipere, nisi forte de consilio proprii sacerdotis, ob aliquam rationabilem causam, ad tempus ab ejus perceptione duxerit abstinendum.

THE right to receive Communion is enjoyed by every baptized person, unless there is a legitimate prohibition to the contrary.[1] For everyone who has received the sacrament of Baptism is entitled, *de jure divino,* to receive the Eucharist inasmuch as Baptism is the spiritual door to the rest of the sacraments. Furthermore, those who have been baptized have not only the right to communicate but also an obligation, which emanates from the mandate of Christ: "Unless you eat the flesh of the Son of Man, you shall not have life in you." To secure a qualified compliance with this divine command, the Church has formulated the paschal precept which obliges all the faithful to receive the Eucharist once a year, and that during the paschal season.

In a canonical treatment of this ecclesiastical law, obviously the first question which suggests itself is: whom does the obligation bind? The two main conditions are given in the canon quoted above, namely, baptism and the use of reason. These two conditions determine the subject of the precept. Furthermore, in some instances the Church has restricted the right of certain classes, who otherwise comply with the conditions demanded by the law, to receive the Eucharist. Finally, special emphasis must be placed on the question of children as subjects of the precept, for many problems must be settled in regard to their relation to the ecclesiastical obligation. By such a process of elimination, a definite and clear idea will be ac-

[1] Can. 853. Cf. Blat, lib. III *de Rebus,* p. I, *de sac. Eucharistiae,* p. 186.

quired of the conditions which bring a person within the scope of the precept.

Article I.—The Condition of Baptism

By reason of the divine law, every human being who has received the Baptism of water is entitled to receive the Eucharist, and *a fortiori,* becomes a subject of the ecclesiastical law, provided, of course, that the other conditions are fulfilled. It is important to remember that it is the Baptism of water, not the Baptism of desire or blood, which is a determining factor in constituting one a subject of the ecclesiastical obligation of receiving Communion once a year.[2] As a consequence, catechumens are not bound by the precept; and as a matter of fact, in the early Church they were strictly excluded from receiving the Eucharist.[3] Cappello[4] raises the question whether those who are doubtfully baptized are bound by the precept. If the right to receive Communion can be established, the person in question cannot claim exemption from the obligation on the grounds that "*lex dubia non obligat,*" (a doubtful law does not bind), for the obligation is a natural consequent of the right. In practice, every effort should be made to dispel the doubt, and if the doubt still remains, then the person concerned is to be considered as capable of receiving Communion.[5]

Article II.—The Use of Reason

The second factor in determining the subject of the paschal precept is the use of reason. The use of reason has always been considered as essential for incurring the obligation of any law, and so also in the case of the paschal precept. In general, then, it may be said that those who do not have the use of this faculty are in no wise bound by this law. This is an ecclesiastical restriction on the right to receive the Eucharist, for Christ never excluded either infants or

[2] Gasparri, *De SS. Eucharistia,* n. 1118; De Lugo, *de sacram. Eucharistiae,* disp. XIII, n. 4.

[3] Bona, *Rerum Liturgicarum,* I, cap. 16; Schanz, *Die Lehre von den hl. Sakramenten der Kirche,* n. 35; Gasparri, *op. cit.,* n. 1118.

[4] *De Sacramentis,* I, n. 460.

[5] Durieux-Dolphin, *The Eucharist, Law and Practice,* p. 165.

those adults who did not enjoy the use of reason from participating in the sacrament of the Eucharist.

Children who have not attained the use of reason are as a consequence forbidden to receive the Eucharist, and do not come within the scope of the law. The Church has good reason to forbid such children to receive Communion, for reverence towards this sacrament demands that it be received with an appreciation of which children who do not enjoy the use of reason, are incapable.[6] Moreover, the Council of Trent [7] has authoritatively defined that before they attain the use of reason children are under no necessity of receiving Holy Communion, because being regenerated in the laver of Baptism, and embodied in Christ, they have received the grace of adoption, which, at their age, they cannot lose.[8]

A more detailed discussion of this condition as it affects children will be entered into in a later article which will consider the relation of children to the paschal precept. At this point it is only necessary to state the general principle that children who do not enjoy the use of reason, are not obliged to communicate once a year.

Since the use of reason is an essential requisite in the subject of the paschal precept, it follows logically that this law does not bind those who have been completely mentally deranged from birth.[9] This conclusion is confirmed by the Roman Ritual [10] which says:—"Amentibus seu phreneticis communicare non licet." If it is unlawful for the insane to exercise their right to communicate, then obviously they cannot be considered as subject to the obligation of the ecclesiastical law.

Sometimes it happens that their insanity is not general; a person whose reason may be defective on other subjects, might be able to discern the Body of Christ from ordinary food and give it respectful adoration; he might even be able to know the chief mysteries of faith and have a true devotion for the Holy Eucharist. A chaplain will frequently meet such a case in institutions devoted to the

[6] Noldin, *de Sacramentis*, p. 134.

[7] Sess. XXI, *de Communione*, can. 4.

[8] *Conc. Trident., loc. cit.*, cap. 4.

[9] *Perpetuo amentes.*

[10] Tit. IV, c. I, n. 10.

care of the insane. What should be his *modus agendi?* In the first place, there seems to be no reason why the patient should not be treated as an ordinary Christian. In other words, he has a right to communicate, and *a fortiori,* the obligation to do so. But since it is probable that such a person may not advert to his duty to receive Communion during the Easter season, it will be the chaplain's charge to give him an opportunity to communicate in order to discharge his obligation.[11] The solution is otherwise when a person's reason is defective precisely in regard to the Eucharist. In such an instance, he is not only not bound by the paschal precept, but is forbidden to receive the Eucharist.[12]

Frequently it will happen that those who have become insane after reaching the use of reason, will have lucid intervals. Most authors grant that their right to communicate is restored if they are in danger of death, but deny that there is any obligation to receive the Eucharist if such an interval came, for example, during the paschal season. The Code does not discuss the question directly, but, as Cappello [13] points out, a very good argument can be deduced from canon 854, which refers to the Communion of children. The Roman Ritual [14] lays down the following principle:—"Amentibus et phreneticis communicare non licet; licebit tamen, si quando habeant lucida intervalla et devotionem ostendant, dum in eo statu manent, si nullum indignitatis periculum adsit." In other words, provided that there is no danger of irreverence, and granted that such a person has some appreciation of the Sacrament and the requisite knowledge, there is no restriction on his right to communicate. However, if there is no impediment to his reception of the Eucharist, there seems no reason why he does not also incur the obligation.[15] It may be objected that such a person cannot have the necessary knowledge and appreciation to receive the Sacrament during these periods of sanity; but that seems to be a question of fact rather than of doctrine, and hence cannot militate against this

[11] Aertnys-Damien, *Theologia Moralis,* II, n. 137.

[12] Cappello, *op. cit.,* n. 463; Gasparri, *op. cit.,* n. 1123.

[13] *Op. cit.,* n. 463.

[14] Tit. IV, cap. I, n. 10.

[15] Cappello, *loc. cit.*

opinion. In the last analysis, it will be the problem of the chaplain to decide whether the lucidity in such intervals is sufficient to restore to the patient his right and even his obligation to communicate. The same holds true of imbeciles, idiots from birth, or those who have become so after having had the full use of reason. The common opinion is that they are to be given Communion only at Easter time and at the hour of death.[16]

Although, strictly speaking, the question of deaf-blind-mutes should not be discussed in this article, still, since in some instances they are likened to infants, it was considered proper at this point to discuss their relation to the paschal precept.

Are mutes, who are both blind and deaf, to be considered as bound by the paschal precept? In order to answer this question, a distinction should be made. If this condition existed before they attained the use of reason, and they have never received instruction, there can be no question of an obligation to communicate during the paschal season because in such circumstances they are likened to infants.[17] On the other hand, if they have received some kind of instruction and education, the matter cannot be settled so readily. Some authors [18] claim that it is impossible for this class of people to acquire the knowledge and devotion requisite for admittance to the Eucharist. Gasparri, for example, holds that even if a deaf mute were to bless himself, genuflect, or otherwise give external evidence of an appreciation of the Sacrament, still such signs might only be a mere imitation of the conduct of others, and consequently in no wise an indication of appreciation or knowledge of the Real Presence. Perhaps such an opinion would have been the correct one in the past. However, present day methods of imparting knowledge to deaf and blind mutes are vastly improved over those of a few decades ago, and consequently, it is entirely within the range of probability that such persons can acquire a sufficient knowledge and devotion for the Eucharist to make them fit subjects of the paschal precept.[19] This conclusion is still more applicable to deaf-

[16] Genicot, *Institutiones Theologiae Moralis,* II, n. 190.

[17] Noldin, *de Sacramentis,* p. 134; Cappello, *de Sacramentis,* I, n. 465.

[18] Gasparri, *de SS. Eucharistia,* n. 1123; Noldin, *op. cit.,* p. 135.

[19] Prümmer, *Manuale Theologiae Moralis,* III, n. 143; Cappello, *op. cit.,* n. 465.

mutes. Of course, it cannot be expected that they will acquire the necessary knowledge and devotion for the reception of Communion as quickly as children who have attained the use of reason, and consequently for them, the obligation of the ecclesiastical law will not begin as early. The chaplain or those in charge will have to make the final decision on their capacity to assume this obligation.

Article III.—Spiritual Dispositions

In canon 859 it is very clearly stated that only the faithful who have attained the use of reason, are bound by the paschal precept. The word "faithful" immediately excludes heretics and schismatics from consideration as subjects of the obligation. For, elsewhere [20] the Code has laid down the rule that it is forbidden to administer the Sacraments to heretics or schismatics, even though they err in good faith, unless they have first rejected their errors and have been reconciled to the Church.

The ecclesiastical law of communicating once a year is so general that it binds all the faithful who have attained the use of reason. Consequently no one is excused from its obligation, even though he be an invalid, prisoner, excommunicate, or public sinner.[21] In the case of the sick and those who are incarcerated in prisons, it is the duty of the pastor or the chaplain to give them an opportunity to comply with the precept. If the pastor or chaplain are remiss in this matter, the imputability for the violation of the law rests with them rather than with the invalid and the prisoner.[22]

The Church forbids all sinners to receive the Eucharist, but she commands absolute exclusion from the Holy Table of all persons who are publicly unworthy of it. The Code [23] names as publicly unworthy the excommunicated, interdicted, or notoriously infamous. In this last category may be included concubinarians, prostitutes, and those who are known to be carrying on an immoral business.[24]

[20] Canon 731.

[21] Cappello, *op. cit.*, n. 475; Gasparri, *de SS. Eucharistia*, n. 1165.

[22] Gasparri, *ibidem.*

[23] Canon 2232.

[24] Ayrinhac, *Legislation on the Sacraments*, p. 169; Blat, *Commentarium Textus Codicis Juris Canonici*, III, n. 173.

On the one hand, the obligation of the paschal precept is not suspended for this class of the faithful merely because they have lost their right to communicate; on the other hand, priests are forbidden to give the Eucharist to public sinners. How are these two obligations to be reconciled? In the first place, the sinner must approach a priest and humbly crave absolution in order that he may be able to fulfil the precept.[25] Then he must take the proper steps to recover his right to communicate, namely by an amendment of his life proportioned to the nature of his sins. In some instances this may take some time, but the confessor can extend the time for fulfilling the precept beyond the ordinary limits required by the law, since there is a reasonable cause for the delay.

Article IV.—Children as the Subjects of the Precept

Canon 859. § 1. Omnis utriusque sexus fidelis, postquam ad annos discretionis, idest ad rationis usum, pervenerit, debet semel in anno, saltem in Paschate, Eucharistiae sacramentum recipere. . . .

Canon 854. § 1. Pueris, qui propter aetatis imbecillitatem nondum hujus sacramenti cognitionem et gustum habent, Eucharistia ne ministretur.

It has already been seen that the obligation of receiving Communion at Easter time, as laid down by the Church, applies to all the faithful, as soon as they have reached the age of discretion. This law merely reproduces the command issued by the fourth Council of Lateran. In the past theologians did not agree on the meaning of the phrase, "the age of discretion." Some construed it as meaning the age of puberty; others, as the age when the intellect is sufficiently developed to have an exact idea of the Eucharistic mystery; some fixed that age at twelve years, and as that age permitted the giving to children of a more complete doctrinal education, it was sanctioned in many countries by diocesan regulations. The Church never adopted this practice, and on several occasions the Holy See had expressed disapproval of it. Finally in 1910 the

[25] Cappello, *De Sacramentis,* I, n. 475; Gasparri, *op. cit.*, n. 1165.

Congregation of Sacraments, by the order of Pope Pius X, published the Decree *Quam Singulari* which removed all doubts and put to an end to controversies on the subject, authoritatively deciding that the age of discretion required both for Confession and Communion is the time when the child begins to reason, that is, about the seventh year, and that from this time on the obligation of both Confession and Communion exists for the child.

§1. *The Age for Communion*

Between the two canons quoted above there is a sharp distinction. In the former it is stated that from the time he attains the use of reason, each and every Catholic is bound to receive Holy Communion at least once in the year. In the latter, the Code teaches that children who by reason of their age have not yet a knowledge and desire for this Sacrament, should not be given Holy Communion. In other words, the use of reason is made the point of demarcation at which the child is no longer forbidden to receive the Eucharist, and incurs the obligation of the paschal precept.

By reason of these two canons, it is no longer correct to teach that it is a question of years which determines the ecclesiastical obligation of communicating once a year. It is no longer a question of years which resolves a child's relation to the paschal precept; it is simply the use of reason which determines whether or not the child comes within the scope of canon 859. If the Code uses the old phrase *"annos discretionis"* of the Lateran Council, it does so for two reasons; first, out of reverence for the Council; and secondly, because the canonist or theologian can no longer interpret it at his own caprice, since it admits of only one interpretation, namely, the use of reason, which is given it by the Code itself.[26]

Notwithstanding the clear language in which the law is now couched, there are still writers who maintain that it is the number of years, rather than the use of reason, which determines the capacity of the child to assume the obligation of the paschal precept.[27] Sim-

[26] Cf. Cerato, *L' agitata Questione sulla età del fanciullo e la Communione di precetto,* p. 6.

[27] E. g., Augustine, *A Commentary,* IV, 227. He writes:—"But no obligation to admit them before the seventh year can be read into the text, nor has

ilar to this opinion is that which holds that the ecclesiastical law does not oblige the child not yet seven years of age, who already has been admitted to the reception of the Eucharist.

The importance of reaching a definite decision on this question is evident. It is of supreme interest to the pastor or confessor to know if a child, not yet seven years of age, is bound by this law of the Church. Many priests still have the most serious difficulty in reconciling themselves to a full compliance with the law in this regard. One does not have to seek far for the source of their difficulty. It arises from a real scruple whether the child can possess that fitting devotion which is required for the reception of the most august of the sacraments.

Yet in deciding that children become subjects of the paschal precept as soon as they attain the use of reason, the Church did not act rashly nor without mature deliberation.[28] Nor was a new doctrine promulgated, but there was had only the restoration of the ancient discipline.[29]

The use of reason is now the determining factor in resolving the status of children in regard to the paschal precept. When does the child attain this use of reason? In the first place, it is impossible to fix definitely the age of discretion, for the verification of this condition will depend upon several factors, for example, upon the mental development of the child, the maturity of its judgment, and the care expended in its education.[30] Individual circumstances must also be taken into consideration, for children differ with regard to natural talents, mental capacity as well as moral disposition. Home training, the surroundings in which a child lives, the school which he attends, and divers other factors are apt to influence his

such an obligation been established by the latest decrees." Cerato (*op. cit.*, p. 3) quotes some periodicals in which writers have endeavoured to prove this point.—*Bollettino Ecclesiastico-Veronese*, 1923, pp. 131-134; 169-172; 195-198; *Palestra del Clero*, May, 1923; *Rivista del Clero Italiano*, 1921.

[28] Leading theologians had already held this opinion, for example, St. Thomas, *Summa Theologica*, 3 part., q. 80, a. 9, ad 3; Ledesma *in S. Thom.*, 3. p., q. 80, a. 9, dub. 6; Vasquez, *in 3 p. S. Thom.*, disp. 214, c. 4, n. 43; D' Annibale, *Summula Theologiae Moralis*, III, n. 396.

[29] Cappello, *op. cit.*, n. 834.

[30] Gasparri, *De SS. Eucharistia*, n. 1167; Cappello, *op. cit.*, n. 475.

character and development.[31] Consequently, a consistent norm cannot be established for the simple reason that intellectual development is not governed by fixed laws. Accordingly, it is not at all unusual for a precocious child to acquire the use of its reasoning powers at the tender age of five, while the mental development of another child may be retarded to the age of ten.[32] The only general rule is that which is given by the decree *"Quam Singulari"* [33] namely,—"The age of discretion both for Confession and Communion is the time when the child begins to reason, that is about the seventh year, more or less. From this time on the obligation of satisfying the precept of both Confession and Communion begins." As has been said, it is difficult to know at what time the child begins to reason. However, there are various facts which will indicate the incipient use of the intellect. If the child begins to recognize his parents or relatives, or can translate his thinking processes and emotions into speech, or is able to distinguish good from evil, then it is safe to assume that he is exercising his reasoning powers. Since this discretion evidently has degrees, it follows that the Church does not require in children the full use of reason; it suffices if they have a *certain* use of reason [34] which permits them to distinguish good from evil, and which consequently makes it possible for them to commit sin.

The question has been raised whether the use of reason demanded by the law must be such that a child is capable of committing a mortal sin. Such a question was proposed to the Holy See by the Bishop of Norcia, but the Commission for the Authentic Interpretation of the Code gave an answer which evaded the issue, and simply said that the use of reason required for receiving Holy Communion is sufficiently specified in canon 854, §2, 3, and for Confession in canon 906.[35] In other words, if the child can acquire a knowledge of the fundamental principles of faith and a reverence and devotion in fitting harmony with its years, then it will have

[31] Schulze, *A Manual of Pastoral Theology*, p. 76.

[32] Cappello, *De Aetate Admittendorum ad Primam Communionem Eucharisticam*, p. 35.

[33] Rule I—*A. A. S.*, II (1910), 581.

[34] St. Thomas, *Summa Theologica*, III, q. 80, art. 9, ad 3.

[35] Feb. 24, 1920; AkKR, CI, 68 (1921).

the use of reason which the Code demands. The child's capacity to commit mortal sin has nothing to do with this knowledge and devotion, and probably that is why the Commission simply referred to the respective canons on Holy Communion and Confession.[36]

It is commonly objected that a child who is just beginning to acquire the use of reason, is incapable of assuming the grave obligation of the paschal precept because of its tender years. While it is true that the failure to comply with the precept will not carry with it the same degree of imputability as it would in the case of an adult, still the Code[37] has provided for this contingency by sharing the responsibility for the fulfilment of the law with those persons, who by nature or by law, are directly concerned with the moral education of the child.[38]

§2. *Further Confirmation*

To leave no room for the former controversies, the Code declared that the child on attaining the use of reason becomes a subject of the paschal precept. Ordinarily the child will reach this stage of its mental development about the seventh year, but there is nothing absolute about this indication; the use of reason may come before or after this age, and it is this, and this alone which

[36] Woywod, *A Practical Commentary on the Code of Canon Law,* I, 414. Cappello (*De Sacramentis,* I, n. 475) refers to a response given by Cardinal Gasparri on this point. According to the reply, the use of reason in question is such as is sufficient for the commission of venial sin; in order to be permitted to receive Communion, the child need not be capable of committing a mortal sin. It is true that many authors, with St. Thomas (*Summa Theologica,* p. I, IIae, q. 89, a. 6), do not admit that a child is capable of committing a venial sin before he is capable of committing a mortal sin. But this only goes to show that the child is not expected to have the full use of reason.

In this connection, another point is worthy of comment. It is plain that it would be contrary to the mind and will of the Church to make a distinction between the age required for Confession and the age required for Communion. There is only one age of reason; and this age marks the commencement of the obligation to go to Confession and to receive the Eucharist.

[37] Canon 860.

[38] Cerato, *L'Agitata Questione sulla età del fanciullo et la Communione di precetto,* p. 9.

conditions the precept and the right to communicate. However, notwithstanding the clear language in which the law is couched, a question was proposed to the Commission for the Authentic Interpretation of the Code by the Archbishop of New York and the Bishop of Valleyfield. The question and the response are worthy of note:

Utrum pueri, qui etsi septimum aetatis annum nondum expleverunt, tamen ob aetatem discretionis seu usum rationis ad primam Communionem admissi jam fuerint, teneantur duplici praecepto confessionis saltem semel in anno et Communionis semel in anno, saltem in Paschate?

E. mus Card. Petrus Gasparri Commissionis Praeses respondet; *Affirmative.* Et ratio in aperto est. Nam quamvis canon 12 statuat: "legibus mere ecclesiasticis non tenentur . . . qui licet rationis usum assecuti, septimum aetatis annum nondum expleverunt," subdit tamen; "nisi aliud jure expresse caveatur." Jamvero in can. 859, §1, et canon 906 expresse cavetur: "omnis utriusque sexus fidelis postquam ad annos discretionis, idest ad usum rationis pervenerit" etc.

P. Cardinalis Gasparri,
Aloisius Sincero, Secr.[39]

This answer should have settled definitely all controversy on this point. For herein is evident confirmation of the use of reason as the determining factor in subjecting the child to the obligation of the paschal precept, regardless of whether he had completed his seventh year or not. It is true that according to canon 12, ecclesiastical laws do not bind children until they have completed their seventh year, even though they may enjoy the use of reason before that time. But this canon also contains the restriction "unless the law expressly stipulates the contrary." This response declares that this contrary stipulation is found in canon 859. The reason is obvious. The precept of Easter Communion is at one and the same time of divine and ecclesiastical law, for on the one hand, Christ commanded men to receive Communion, and on the other, it is the Church which explains and defines when this Communion must be received.

Nevertheless, the authenticity of this response has been seriously

[39] *Jus Pontificium,* I, p. 5; Perez, *Decisiones Pontificiae ad Canones Codicis Juris Canonici,* p. 43.

questioned.[40] The attack on its authenticity rests mainly on the fact that the answer was not published in the official organ of the Holy See, the *Acta Apostolicae Sedis.* However, as Blat [41] points out, there was no need for its publication in the official organ since it was merely declaratory.[42]

The argument against the intrinsic worth of the response is more specious. In the reply of Cardinal Gasparri, the obligation of annual Confession as well as the obligation of the paschal precept, is considered. According to the critics, the obligation to approach the tribunal of Penance does not begin with the dawn of reason, but is incurred only when the child commits sin. According to this theory, if a child were to reach the age of twenty without committing sin, the obligation of annual Confession would not yet urge. They conclude that since this serious mistake is made in the first part of the response, there is good reason to doubt the correctness of the second part which refers to the annual Communion.

This farfetched conclusion is in large part due to the disregard between the law and its obligation, and the subject of the law and its observance. The fallacious reasoning will become evident by the use of an illustration. A state regulation in Pennsylvania makes it unlawful to drive faster than thirty-five miles an hour on the highway. When a driver receives his license he becomes a subject of this ruling. The obligation commences for the driver, not after he has committed his first speeding offense, but from the moment he received his license to drive a car. In just the same way, the child becomes a subject of the law of annual Confession as soon as he attains the use of reason, not after he commits his first offense against God. This comparison is by no means perfect, but it will serve to bring out the point. Since both of these objections against the authenticity and the intrinsic worth of the response are without substance, there should be no hesitation in accepting it as further confirmation of the use of reason as the deciding element in bringing children within the scope of the law of annual Communion.

Still another argument may be drawn from the Code itself in

[40] Cf. Cerato, *op. cit.*, p. 16.

[41] *Commentarium Textus Codicis Juris Canonici,* III, 195.

[42] Canon 17, §2.

confirmation of this opinion. In the Code there is no special law which prescribes a time within which the First Communion should be made. However, the pastor is asked to see that children who have attained the use of reason and possess the necessary dispositions, should partake of this divine nourishment as soon as possible.[43] On the other hand, it is his strict duty to watch that children do not approach the Holy Table before they have attained the use of reason.[44] In both instances the Code uses the expression, *usus rationis,* and this, coupled with the fact that the same words are employed in canon 859, proves beyond question that the attaining of the use of reason marks the beginning of the obligation of the paschal precept.

It may not be amiss at this point to sketch briefly in the form of conclusions what has gone before. Therefore:

(1) The element which determines the status of the child in relation to the paschal precept is the use of reason.

(2) The use of reason which brings the child within the obligation of this law is that which children as a rule possess about the age of seven years. Ordinarily, therefore, children are held by this obligation in their seventh year.

(3) If it can be demonstrated with moral certainty that an exceptional child at the age of five or six, has reached the stage of mental development common to the ordinary child in his seventh year, then this exceptional child is obliged to make the Easter Communion. If, on the contrary, in an exceptional case, it is discovered that a child does not enjoy this use of reason on the completion of his seventh year, he is not bound to comply with the paschal precept. Furthermore, if the child in his tenth year did not enjoy the use of reason common to children in the seventh year, he does not come within the scope of the law.[45]

(4) If, after a searching investigation, there still remains a reasonable doubt of the child's having attained the use of reason, the following distinction must be made:

A. If the child has not completed his seventh year, the presump-

[43] Canon 854, §5.

[44] *Ibid.*

[45] Canon 12.

tion is against his having attained the use of reason.[46] Consequently, such a child ordinarily is not considered as a subject of the precept.

B. On the other hand, if the child has completed his seventh year, generally he becomes subject to the ecclesiastical obligation.[47] For children, according to canon 88, are assumed to attain the use of reason on the completion of their seventh year by a presumption of the law. This presumption will not hold if there is proof to the contrary since "*presumptio cedit veritati.*" This is the only case in which the age of the child is taken into consideration. Since the child usually (*ex communiter contingentibus*) reaches the age of discretion on or about the completion of his seventh year, the Code has very wisely taken advantage of this fact to guide the parent or confessor when otherwise it is extremely difficult to decide whether the child has reached the stage of mental development desired by the law.

§3. *The Knowledge Required by the Code*

> **Canon 854. § 3. Extra mortis periculum plenior cognitio doctrinae christianae et accuratior praeparatio merito exigitur, ea scilicet, qua ipsi fidei saltem mysteria necessaria necessitate medii ad salutem pro suo captu percipiant, et devote pro suae aetatis modulo ad sanctissimam Eucharistiam accedant.**

Heretofore, nothing was said about the preparation required for the reception of the paschal precept, not because the child should not approach the altar suitably prepared, but the better to express how the child becomes a subject of the law by the mere fact of having acquired the use of reason.[48] The lack of such preparation, which must be imputed to those responsible for the child's welfare, should be considered as an excusing, rather than an exempting cause.

[46] Canon 88, §3; O'Donnell, "The Admission of Children to Holy Communion"—*I. E. R.*, II, 644 (1913); Cerato, *op. cit.*, p. 7.

[47] Vermeersch-Creusen, *Epitome Juris Canonici,* II, n. 118; Woywod, *op. cit.*, I, 409; Cappello, *op. cit.*, I, n. 475.

[48] Cerato, *L'Agitata Questione sulla età del fanciullo e la Communione di precetto,* p. 5.

This distinction is important since it places the preparation for the reception of Communion in its proper relation to the primary and more important condition, the use of reason.

The Code is more stringent in its requirements than the decree "Quam Singulari" for it lays more stress on the knowledge and preparation demanded of the candidate for Communion. The reason for this insistence on a "fuller knowledge of Christian doctrine and more careful preparation" is obvious when one considers the motive which inspired the "Quam Singulari." That memorable decree was directed primarily against the deplorable abuse of late Communions which resulted when theologians, influenced by the Jansenistic heresy, insisted upon an age, a knowledge of religion, and a degree of piety far beyond what was necessary. To eliminate such abuses in the future, the decree formulated rules which lent themselves to a wider interpretation than was intended. Some, it seems, thought it would suffice to teach children that the Eucharist was not a common food. Besides this, the children were to be instructed that the state of grace was necessary for the reception of Communion. All this, they claimed, could be explained in a few days' or even hours' instruction.[49] With a view to checking such extreme interpretations of the decree, the Code emphasized the knowledge and devotion which are required in order that the child may incur the obligation of the paschal precept.[50]

When a child is in danger of death, it will suffice if he is able to distinguish the Eucharist from common and material bread.[51] Outside the danger of death, the Church expects a fuller knowledge and a more complete preparation for the reception of Communion, and until this knowledge has been acquired, the child is excused from the obligation of the paschal precept.[52] The knowledge demanded is not that of the whole Christian doctrine, but simply of the truths necessary as absolute means of salvation.[53] But it would

[49] Schulze, *A Manual of Pastoral Theology*, p. 81.

[50] Vermeersch-Creusen, *op. cit.*, II, n. 118; Noldin, *De Sacramentis*, III, 141.

[51] Jorio, *La Communione Agl' Infermi*, p. 11.

[52] Cerato, *op. cit.*, p. 8.

[53] Cappello, *De Aetate Admittendorum ad Primam Communionem Eucharisticam*, p. 40; Ayrinhac, *Legislation on the Sacraments*, p. 164; Curran, *The Eucharistic Life*, p. 219.

be erroneous to say that the Church demands a complete knowledge of the truths of religion, or even a comparatively deep knowledge, or a preparation which is ordinarily incompatible with the frivolity of tender years. The Code simply demands, as did the decree "Quam Singulari," that children know these truths *pro suo captu,* that is, according to their capacity for understanding.[54]

What are the essential truths and mysteries which are required for the reception of the Eucharist? M. Besson sums them up in a manner which leaves nothing to be desired:

> Let us suppose the case of a child brought up, I do not say in pious or very fervent surrounding, but, at all events, averagely Christian ones. It knows that God exists, and that there is but One, the best of all Beings, that Father Who is in heaven; to Him the child is made pray morning and evening, and when attending church. It has been told that this God punishes the bad and rewards the good. It has heard about heaven, where dwell those angels and saints whose images it sees in the church. It has heard of hell, where people burn with the demons. The names of the Father, Son, and Holy Ghost have been often on its lips when making the sign of the Cross, and there is no difficulty in teaching it the fact that each of these Three Persons is God, and yet that there is but one God. There is the image of the Infant Jesus, before whose crib the child kneels at Christmas time, or Who is represented in statues of Holy Mary as held in His Mother's arms; the crucifix, the visit to the Altar of Repose on Holy Thursday—these will have taught it about the God-Man Who came from heaven and died upon the Cross for our sins. Here we can see that—in a fragmentary way, it is true, yet with considerable clearness—all the necessary truths have been conveyed to the child by hearing and by the sight of everyday objects. This is sufficient.[55]

The essential truths are contained in this excerpt. While it is true that some theologians [56] teach that a knowledge of the Blessed

In this connection the advice of Benedict XIV is worthy of note. He instructed bishops to admonish pastors not to admit anyone to Holy Communion who did not know the more important articles of faith, and chapters of Christian doctrine, and the strength and efficacy of the Blessed Eucharist." *"Etsi Minime,"* 7 Feb., 1742, n. 9.—*Fontes,* n. 324.

[54] St.Thomas, *Summa Theologica,* p. 3, q. 80, a. 9, ad 3.

[55] *N. R. Théol.* (1910), p. 658.

[56] Cf. Cappello, *De Sacramentis,* I, n. 462; Curran, *The Eucharistic Life,* p. 220.

Trinity and the Incarnation is not absolutely necessary for salvation, still it is not too much to demand that the child should have some knowledge of their existence.[57]

§4. *The Devotion Required by the Code*

Besides the requisite knowledge, there is still required on the part of the child some desire and devotion for the Eucharist. As regards devotion, the Code demands that the child shall receive Communion with piety, it is true, but with a piety which is in proportion to its age (*pro suae aetatis modulo*). The Latin diminutive indicates very plainly that even very imperfect dispositions will suffice, and that the child is not to be required to manifest a recollection and ardour of which it is incapable.

Vermeersch [58] defines *gustus* or desire as a sincere will to receive Christ for Himself, and not to please parents or to imitate adults. Sometimes it is difficult to determine whether the child is actuated by such a motive, or whether it displays enough devotion to merit the reception of the Eucharist. In such cases the following hints should be kept in mind. First, it should be remembered that thoughtlessness and forgetfulness are the inevitable associates of childhood, and that one pure act of love and adoration will more than compensate for these imperfections. Secondly, it should not be forgotten that these faults are viewed through the spectrum of age and experience—mature advantages to which the child has yet to be introduced. Finally, Christ does not require of the child more than it can give Him; He only expects that its piety and devotion be commensurate with its years.

[57] Gennari, *Sulla Età della prima Communione dei fanciulli*, p. 8; Ayrinhac, *op. cit.*, p. 164; McNicholas, "The Age of Children for First Communion"—*A. E. R.*, 43 (1910), 485.

[58] *Theologia Moralis*, III, n. 391.

CHAPTER IV

THE RIGHTS AND DUTIES OF THE PARENTS, CONFESSOR, PASTOR, AND TEACHERS

Canon 860. Obligatio praecepti sumendae, quae impuberes gravat, in eos quoque ac praecipue recidit, qui ipsorum curam habere debent, idest in parentes, tutores, confessarium, institutores et parochum.

Canon 854. § 4. De sufficienti puerorum dispositione ad primam communionem judicium esto sacerdoti a confessionibus eorumque parentibus aut iis qui loco parentum sunt.

Article I.—Preliminary Survey

Although the law of annual Communion applies to children as soon as they reach the age of discretion, it does not follow that they may receive this Sacrament immediately upon arriving at this stage of their mental development. There remains for them to prepare, to acquire the knowledge of the Eucharist and of the truths necessary by necessity of means required for its proper reception, and to develop the dispositions of respect and devotion demanded of them. This preparation the child cannot make unaided, but the Code has provided for this contingency in canon 860. This canon reminds parents, guardians, confessors, directors of school, and pastors, of the obligation incumbent upon them to see that the *impuberes* entrusted to their care, comply with the paschal precept. Puberty commences for boys with the fourteenth, and for girls with the twelfth year.[1] After that age the obligation, if not morally, ceases at least juridically, for the classes of persons named in the canon.[2] This obligation, moreover, is not to be regarded lightly since the object of the law is grave.[3]

[1] Canon 81, §2.

[2] Augustine, *A Commentary*, IV, 239.

[3] Cerato, *L'Agitata Questione sulla età del fanciullo e la Communione di precetto*, p. 9; Cappello, *De Sacramentis*, I, n. 534.

Strictly speaking, there is no question of right as applying either to the parents, or the confessor, or the pastor. A right exists only as regards the child; as soon as he reaches the age of reason and possesses the required dispositions, he has the right and the duty to receive the Eucharist. But, left to himself, he would not advert to his obligations in the matter; it therefore pertains to those who have charge of him to see that he receives Communion.

In canon 860, the parents are mentioned first, and after them, the guardians, confessor, teachers, and the pastor. This order is not arbitrary; it is based on a definite principle of responsibility. Parents are primarily responsible for the education of their children; hence theirs is the principal obligation in the matter. Then follow the confessor, teacher, and the pastor in the order mentioned. The pastor appears among this group because it belongs to him to see that his parishioners do not neglect the laws of the Church. But he is named last, because his intervention is only needed in default of the other persons mentioned as being "in charge" of the child.

It should be remembered that the word *parentes* includes not only the father and the mother, but also the grandparents.[4] Moreover, whatever is said in the following article about parents, applies equally to guardians, since the parental power and obligations are supposed to devolve upon them.[5] Consequently it will not be necessary to enter into a separate discussion of their rights and obligations towards the child who has become subject to the paschal precept.

Article II.—The Parents

§1. *The Right to Decide on the Child's Fitness*

The child, by the very fact of his being baptized, has a right to the Holy Eucharist; consequently, his admission to the Holy Table cannot be, in the strict sense of the word, a permission to receive Communion; it can be nothing more than a simple declaration made to him concerning his right. Moreover, when the child has attained the imperfect use of reason of which the Code speaks,

[4] Canon 750, §2, 2°; Cappello, *op. cit.*, n. 534.

[5] Benedict XIV, Ep. *"Postremo mense,"* 28 Feb. 1747—*Fontes*, n. 377.

he incurs the obligation of satisfying the paschal precept. Since children, however, do not generally advert to their rights and obligations in this matter, and since there would be numerous mistakes made if they were left to decide their own course, it is imperative that there should be someone endowed with authority to make a decision or declaration as to the verification of the various conditions required by the law, before the child can receive the Eucharist. Who is to make this declaration? the parents, the pastor or the confessor? This has been a much controverted question in the past, but since the Code, it has been considerably clarified.

That the parents have a right to judge the fitness of their child to receive Communion, has never been questioned. For, by reason of their natural office, they are charged with the proper education of the child's mind and will, and hence, they are obliged to acquaint him with the precepts of both the divine and ecclesiastical law.[6]

This point is brought out very well by the Roman Catechism: "As for the age at which the sacred Mysteries are to be given to children, none can better decide than the father and the priest to whom they make their confessions; to these (the parents of the child and the confessor) it belongs to ascertain by examining the children whether these have arrived at some understanding (*cognitionem aliqualem*) and have some appreciation of this admirable Sacrament."[7] The decree *"Quam Singulari"*[8] following the Roman Catechism, also decided that the parents and the confessor were the proper persons to decide on the child's fitness for the reception of the Eucharist. The Code has adopted the same rule, with this difference however, that it names the confessor before the parents. This does not necessarily imply priority of right for the confessor, but perhaps indicates the greater importance his decision will usually have.[9] The judgment to be made bears on the mental development

[6] Cappello, *De Aetate Admittendorum ad Primam Communionem Eucharisticam*, p. 42; Gennari, *Sulla Età della prima Communione dei Fanciulli*, p. 21.

[7] *Catechismus Romanus*, p. II, c. VI, *de Sac. Eucharistiae*, n. 68.

[8] Rule IV—Cappello, *De Aetate Admittendorum ad Primam Communionem Eucharisticam*, p. 10; *Fontes*, n. 2103.

[9] Ayrinhac, *Legislation on the Sacraments*, p. 165.

of the child, his degree of knowledge, and his moral dispositions. The parents, who come in daily contact with him, can best observe his status in regard to the first two points, but the confessor will have a similar opportunity when the child comes to Confession, and his training and experience will give him a decided advantage over the parents in making a decision. In any case, his position entitles him to make an authoritative declaration on the internal dispositions of the child.

Few parents would dream of admitting their offspring to Communion without first seeking the consent of the parochial clergy, or contemplate a preparation apart from their supervision or active cooperation. Consequently, in practice parents will generally leave the decision entirely in the hands of the confessor or the pastor, either through indifference on their own part, or from regard for the office of the clergy.

§2. *The Obligation of the Parents*

There devolves upon parents, besides the right to make a declaration on the capacity of their child to assume the obligation of the Easter duty, the corresponding duty of seeing that he complies with this precept when an affirmative declaration has been made.[10] They sin gravely when they know the child is ready to assume the obligation, but refuse to allow him to approach the altar during the paschal season.[11] Parents who are thus responsible for

[10] Gennari, "Circa il divieto dei genitori sulla prima communione de 'loro figli," *Il Monitore Ecclesiastico,* III (ser. 3), 1911, p. 127.

[11] On November 30, 1910, in the *Monitore Ecclesiastico,* Cardinal Gennari gave the following decisions:

When the child who has reached the age of reason does not go to Confession, and does not receive Communion, the following persons are guilty of sin (except, of course, when there are excusing circumstances):

1.—The child himself, in the measure in which he evinces malice in his abstention. Ordinarily this would not be grave.

2.—The parents; in neglecting to see, either on their own behalf or through someone else, that their children fulfil their obligation, they sin mortally against natural piety.

3.—The confessors commit, in this case, two mortal sins, one against the formal precept of the Decree (today, against the law as expressed in the Code), and the other against charity.

the omission of the paschal Communion by their child, are just as guilty as if they omitted their own Easter duty.[12]

Article III.—The Confessor

The Fourth Lateran Council used the words *proprii sacerdotis* in deciding who was to settle the various questions relative to the paschal precept. At first, canonists interpreted this phrase to include only the bishop and the pastor, but in the course of time, they admitted that it also could include the confessor.[13] As a result, the confessor was acknowledged to be juridically competent to decide all the questions which might arise in connection with the Easter Communion, including the difficult one of a child's capacity to assume the obligation of the paschal precept. Such an interpretation was but proper, because, with the possible exception of the parents, the confessor is in a position to know best the intimate sentiments of the child and to judge of the development of his intellect. In the course of time, however, custom limited the powers of the confessor because the reception of the First Communion became a solemn parochial function, in connection with which the pastor claimed definite rights. The decree *"Quam Singulari"* [14] restored to him his former privileges, privileges which have been recognised and strengthened by the Code.

It has been noted already [15] that the Code places the confessor before the parents in the question of judging the child's fitness as a candidate for the reception of the Easter Communion. This brings

4.—Teachers are bound, *in solidum et sub gravi,* together with the parents, by virtue of the quasi-contract which binds them in justice, to enable the children to fulfil their duties.

5.—Pastors also commit mortal sin in the same circumstances.—Gennari, "Circa la colpa e la pena dei fanciulli che, giunti all' uso di ragione, non vanno alla sacra mensa," *Il Monitore Ecclesiastico,* II (1910), 427.

[12] In Confirmation of this opinion, Ferreres cites a decision of the Roman Council of 1725: "Peccantne non communicantes, si debitam aetatem attigerint? . . . si ex defectu patris aut matris alteriusve, qui ad dandam instructionem obligatur, hi peccant mortaliter," *Razon y Fe,* LI (1910), 522.

[13] Many, *Praelectiones de Missa,* p. 306.

[14] Rule IV—Cappello, *De Aetate Admittendorum ad Primam Communionem Eucharisticam,* p. 10; *Fontes,* n. 2103.

[15] Article II.

up the question of the relation between the confessor and the parents in this matter.

Canon 854, §4 states that it belongs to the confessor and to the parents or guardians to judge if the child complies with all the conditions necessary for the reception of the Eucharist. Does this mean that the consent of both is required, or can the confessor act independently of the parents? It is obviously desirable that parents and confessor should act together in admitting the child,[16] but whether it is essential that they should do so is another question. In rule four of the decree *"Quam Singulari"* the words of the decree are: "the father . . . and the confessor," while rule five speaks alternatively of "parents or confessor" as approving the child's admission. Evidently, then, both have the right to judge, but the consent of either is sufficient.[17] This point might, in certain instances, prove important for the child's spiritual interest. Does the Code change this? In view of the fact that the decree, which is incorporated almost without change in the present legislation, does not seem to attach any juridical importance to the conjunction *"and,"* and keeping in mind that canon 860 places the obligation *in solidum* [18] upon several persons, it is entirely reasonable to presume that the former interpretation is still valid.[19]

Since the reception of the annual Communion appertains to the inner court of conscience, the office of the confessor ordinarily should be restricted to the confessional. For it is there that he will discover if the child is ready to become a subject of the paschal precept. When he has done so, his regular procedure then should be to inform the child of this obligation, and impress upon him the necessity of acquainting the parents with his decision. It perhaps may become his duty to instruct the parents also, but this practice is not recommended because it involves the possible violation of the seal of confession.[20]

[16] Vermeersch, "De aetate admittendorum ad primam communionem eucharisticam"—*Periodica,* V, 176 (1913).

[17] Zulueta, *Early First Communion,* p. 71; Vermeersch, *loc. cit.*

[18] Blat, *Commentarium Textus Codicis Juris Canonici,* III, n. 179.

[19] Ayrinhac, *Legislation on the Sacraments,* p. 166.

[20] Vermeersch, "De aetate admittendorum ad primam communionem eucharisticam"—*Periodica,* V (1913), 176; *A. E. R.,* VI (1912), 479.

There have been cases in the past in which parents have refused obstinately to follow the confessor's advice.[21] Should such an *impasse* be reached, the confessor should order his method of procedure in this manner. If the parents deem the child too young to assume the obligation, and have some foundation for their opinion, ordinarily he should not insist too much on the child's receiving the Eucharist.[22] Strictly speaking, the child might receive Communion, but the practical difficulties *hic et nunc* would suspend his obligation for the time being.[23] If, on the other hand, the parents are evidently unreasonable in their attitude, the confessor should prudently endeavour to bring them to a sense of duty. If he fails, the responsibility for the neglect of the ecclesiastical precept would rest with them alone, and his obligation in the matter would cease. The Code has provided for such a contingency in canon 854, §5.

Article IV.—Teachers

Although the duty of instructing children in the fundamental principles of divine and ecclesiastical law falls primarily upon their parents, the latter are free either to fulfil the task themselves, or to commit it to a suitable person of their choice, ordinarily the child's teacher. However, the word *institutores* in canon 860 comprehends not only teachers, but also any person who has to do with the education of the child.[24] When a teacher recognizes that a child has attained sufficient discretion, and the knowledge and devotion demanded by the law, he has a strict obligation to inform the parents of this fact.[25] This obligation arises from the quasi-contract which binds him in justice to enable the children to fulfil their duties.[26]

[21] O'Donnell, "Admission of Children to Communion"—*I. E. R.*, III (1914), 81.

[22] Ayrinhac, *op. cit.*, p. 166.

[23] O'Donnell, *ibid.*

[24] Cappello, *De Aetate Admittendorum ad Primam Communionem Eucharisticam,* p. 42.

[25] Mothon, *Institutions Canoniques,* II, p. 100.

[26] Gennari, "Circa la colpa e la pena dei fanciulli che, giunti all' uso di ragione, non vanno alla sacra mense."—*Il Monitore Ecclesiastico,* II, 427 (1910); Cappello, *De Sacramentis,* I, n. 534.

In the event that the parents or the confessor have neglected their duty in this matter, the teacher may declare directly to the child his obligation to receive the paschal Communion, in virtue of canon 860, because the obligation is *in solidum*.[27] Moreover, the director of a boarding school in which the child may be studying, may disregard any prohibition which is issued by the parents, provided that he is morally certain that the child is juridically competent to fulfil the precept.[28]

Article V.—The Pastor

Before the Code, or, to be accurate, before the promulgation of the decree *"Quam Singulari,"* the right to admit the child to the reception of the Eucharist seems to have been very commonly regarded as falling of right under the exclusive control of those charged with the pastoral care of souls. This impression, at variance with the Roman Catechism, was never justified by the common law.[29] It was due, in no small measure, to the fact that children were apt to be held back and saved up for imposing First Communion celebrations, regardless of the fact that they might long since have been bound by the law of annual Communion. And since the external arrangements for these solemn parochial functions were recognised and confirmed by diocesan and provincial statutes [30] as the right of the pastor, the internal details of the children's preparation and admission to Communion also came to be attributed to the same hands. As a consequence, to an external control of fact, there was added in course of time, an internal one which many mistook for an exclusive right of general control.[31] The Code has clarified the situation by restoring to the confessor and the parents privileges which, although disre-

[27] Blat, *Commentarium Textus Codicis Juris Canonici,* III, n. 179.

[28] Durieux-Dolphin, *The Eucharist, Law and Practice,* p. 189; Prümmer, *Manuale Theologiae Moralis,* III, 159.

[29] O'Donnell, "Has the Parish Priest, as such, the Right to admit to First Communion?"—*I. E. R.*, II, 521 (1913).

[30] O'Donnell, *ibid.*

[31] Zulueta, "The Control of Children's First Communions."—*A. E. R.*, 48, 22 (1913).

garded for a time, were never abrogated.[32] The admission to the First Communion is no longer a strict parochial right, and all contrary rulings whether of provincial or diocesan statutes are abolished,[33] unless an indult has been received from the Holy See.

Although the Code has dispelled the notion that an exclusive right of general control is vested in the pastor, it does not thereby relieve him of all rights and obligations in this matter. Definite duties are committed to his care, and these will be outlined in the course of this article.

§1. *The Vigilance of the Pastor*

> **Canon 854. § 5. Parocho autem est officium advigilandi, etiam per examen, si opportunum prudenter judicaverit, ne pueri ad sacram Synaxim accedant ante adeptum usum rationis vel sine sufficienti dispositione.**

It is the office of the pastor to watch that children do not approach the Holy Table before they have attained the use of reason or without sufficient preparation, and he may examine them if he deems it prudent and opportune. This office assigned to the pastor follows logically from his position as the "spiritual father" of his flock. For thus it belongs to him to see that his parishioners, whether adults or children, do not neglect the laws of the Church.[34]

While, on the one hand, as a result of this office of vigilance entrusted to the pastor, there ensue certain prerogatives, still, on the other, there are certain actions which cannot be justified in virtue of canon 854, §5. To bring out in bolder relief the nature and extent of the pastor's duty in the admittance of children to the Eucharist, these latter will be discussed in the first place.

1. The office of careful supervision as denoted by the word *ad-*

[32] It should be noted that the right of admitting children to their First Communion is not mentioned among the functions reserved by canon 462 to the pastor. Cf. Bouuaert-Simenon, *Manuale Juris Canonici,* n. 571.

[33] Koudelka, *Pastors, Their Rights and Duties according to the New Code of Canon Law,* p. 96.

[34] Micheletti, *Summula Theologiae Pastoralis,* II, 174; Cappello, *De Aetate Admittendorum ad Primam Communionem Eucharisticam,* p. 43.

vigilandi, does not give the pastor a positive or exclusive right to declare the fitness of a child to receive the Eucharist, and *a fortiori,* to assume the obligation of the paschal precept.[35]

2. Provided that he has the consent of the confessor or his parents, a child is in no wise compelled to seek the approval of the pastor before approaching the altar to comply with the paschal precept. In practice, however, it is advisable that the pastor be informed of the child's admission.[36] To some the attribution of the admission to Holy Communion to the confessor and the parents, appeared to weaken the authority of the pastor in his parish, and to give occasion to abuses. To calm these fears, the Holy See authorized some bishops to enact certain regulations which would safeguard the prestige of the pastor.[37] As a result of this legislation, the confessor was to inform the pastor about the children he had declared to be ready to assume the obligation of the paschal precept, and to certify that the necessary conditions of use of reason, knowledge and devotion were fulfilled.

3. The pastor cannot refuse Communion, particularly during the paschal season, to a child whom the confessor or the parents have judged a fit candidate for the Eucharist.[38]

[35] Cappello, *De Sacramentis,* I, n. 530; Ferreres, *Compendium Theologiae Moralis,* II, n. 423.

[36] Cappello, *ibid.;* Genicot-Salsmans, II, n. 210; Cappello, "Nonnullae quaestiones de Confirmatione et prima Communione"—*Periodica,* XVI, 134 (1927); Fanfani, *De Jure Parochorum,* p. 259. In the periodical *Perfice Munus* ([1926], p. 391), Gregori makes the following statement:—"Il fanciullo non può essere ritenuto idoneo alla Communione, sia per sufficiente uso della ragione, sia per sufficienti disposizioni di mente e di volontà, se tale giudizio—da chiunque sia emesso—non e ratificato dal parocco"—quoted by Cappello in his article in the *Periodica.* There is nothing in the Code to justify this opinion, according to which the admission of the child must always include a twofold consultation, the judgment in the internal forum of the confessor and of the parents, and the official appeal to the pastor in the external forum after an examination. Such a claim on Gregori's part is entirely gratuitous, and in fact is opposed to canon 854, §5, in which no mention is made of the ratification of the pastor, or, for that matter, of the pastor at all.

[37] Ayrinhac, *Legislation on the Sacraments,* p. 166; *Conc. Mechlin.,* n. 188 (1920)—quoted by Genicot-Salsmans, *Institutiones Theologiae Moralis,* II, n. 210.

[38] There are exceptions to this rule, but these will be noted later.

For children who have reached the age of discretion, and who are acting on the advice of their parents or confessor, have the same rights and obligations with regard to the Eucharist as anyone else. The exercise of their rights and the discharge of their obligations, does not make them public sinners; and none but public sinners are to be refused the sacraments publicly.[39]

4. The pastor cannot prohibit a child from fulfilling his Easter duty in another parish or in a boarding school. For there is no longer a formal obligation to receive the paschal Communion in one's own parish; [40] besides any confessor is competent to instruct the child as to his obligations.

With these restrictions in mind, it is easier to understand the office of the pastor in regard to the child's admission to the Eucharist and fulfilment of the paschal precept. In general, he should leave to the confessor and the parents the duty of deciding as to the dispositions of the child; his rôle is one of high general surveillance. In other words, this office calls for no more than a general supervision over this as over the other spiritual activities of the parish; however if he were to notice any irregularities, he would have to correct them.[41] But this right of surveillance does not include the right to mix in all the matters he has to supervise.

In the event that abuses in this matter creep into the parish, the Code suggests the means which the pastor should adopt to eradicate them. If he suspects the existence of irregularities, he should make the proper examination, and he may ask the doubtful candidate to submit himself to an examination. The Code, however, by the use of the word *prudenter,* indicates with what prudence and discretion the pastor should use this measure. Only when he has judicious reasons or well-founded suspicions that a particular child is yet incapable of assuming the obligation arising from the paschal precept, may he have recourse to an examination.[42] If he decides in the negative, then his decision must be accepted as final. It must be remem-

[39] Canon 855; Cappello, *De Sacramentis,* I, n. 530.

[40] Cf. chapter V, art. II.

[41] Ayrinhac, *Legislation on the Sacraments,* p. 167; Koudelka, *Pastors, Their Rights and Duties,* p. 96.

[42] Cappello, "Nonnullae quaestiones de Confirmatione et prima Communione," *Periodica,* XVI, 135 (1927).

bered, however, that only in individual instances may he use this prerogative. He cannot impose the obligation of an examination by general rule on all the children as a necessary condition for their reception of the Eucharist.[43]

§2. *The Relation of the Pastor to the Confessor*

Some find it difficult to reconcile the privileges granted to the pastor and the confessor by the Code in this matter.[44] But a close analysis of the problem shows that the apparent conflict does not exist. In the first place, the reception of Communion belongs to the internal forum, and consequently it does not belong to the province of the pastor *as such*[45] but only if he is also the child's confessor. This will happen frequently in smaller Catholic centres where the pastor will be the judge in both the internal and external forum. In such circumstances he will possess an accidental monopoly *in fact,* but not *of right* in all that appertains to the child's Communion, and naturally no conflict will arise.

In a parish where there are one or more assistants, there might be occasion for a clash of prerogatives. But if the prescriptions of the Code are followed faithfully, there need not be a conflict. The judgment or declaration concerning the child's capacity to receive the Eucharist, and, what is more to the point, the Easter Communion, should be made by the confessor in individual cases. On the other hand, the pastor should exercise a policy of general surveillance in the external forum with a view to correcting any abuses which might creep in. Only in isolated instances will his office bring him in contact with the work of the confessor, and then only when he has good reason to suspect that a child does not measure up to the standard demanded by the law. But there cannot be a conflict in such a case, because the jurisdiction of the confessor ceases, and the responsibility for the child's welfare is placed upon the pastor.[46]

[43] Vermeersch-Creusen, *Epitome Juris Canonici,* II, n. 118; Cappello, *De Sacramentis,* I, n. 530; Genicot-Salsmans, *Institutiones Theologiae Moralis,* II, n. 210; Prümmer, *Manuale Theologiae Moralis,* III, n. 211.

[44] Kinane, *I. E. R.,* II (1923), 115.

[45] Zulueta, *Early First Communion,* p. 76.

[46] Vermeersch-Creusen, *Epitome Juris Canonici,* II, n. 118; Cappello, "Nonnullae quaestiones de Confirmatione et prima Communione"—*Periodica,* XVI (1927), 135; *Il Monitore Ecclesiastico,* IV (1920), 157.

§3. *Other Obligations of the Pastor*

Canon 854. §5. . . . Itemque curandi ut usum rationis assecuti et sufficienter dispositi quamprimum hoc divino cibo reficiantur.

Canon 1330. 2°. Peculiari omnino studio, praesertim, si nihil obsit, Quadragesimae tempore, pueros sic instituere ut sancte Sancta primum de altari libent.

It is the pastor's duty to see that those who have attained the use of reason and are sufficiently prepared, are nourished with this divine food as soon as possible. It would be a very grave dereliction of duty on his part if he were remiss in seeing that these children, already juridically competent to assume the obligation, make their Easter duty. How should the pastor proceed in fulfilling this office? Canon 860, it will be recalled, places the obligation of seeing that children satisfy the paschal precept primarily upon the parents. Hence, the pastor in his sermons, before and during the time in which this law of the Church must be obeyed, should remind them of their grave obligations in this matter.[47] If his efforts fail, then in default of the other persons charged with this duty, he should personally make sure that the child receive Communion during the Easter season.[48]

The Code does not determine by any particular prescription a time within which the child must make its First Communion. It only counsels the pastor to see that this Communion be made as soon as possible.[49] What is the precise signification of the word *quamprimum?* Fanfani [50] with good reason claims that it cannot be taken in a strict sense, because it was inserted in the text to guard against the error of the Jansenists, namely, procrastination. Consequently it may be interpreted as meaning within a reasonable time. Authors disagree as to the limits of a reasonable time, but they all

[47] Micheletti, *Summula Theologiae Pastoralis,* II, 174.

[48] Pius X, litt. encycl., "*Acerbo Nimis,*" 15 Apr. 1905—*Fontes,* n. 666; Micheletti, *loc. cit.*

[49] Cerato, *L'Agitata Questione sulla età del fanciullo e la Communione di precetto,* p. 12.

[50] *De Jure Parochorum,* pp. 257, 259.

concur in the opinion that it precludes the deferring of the reception of the Eucharist for more than a year.

This opinion is useful because it is of more particular moment here to know whether the child who has attained the use of reason is obliged to make his Easter duty in the year he becomes subject to the ecclesiastical obligation. For example, is a child who complies with all the conditions demanded by the Code in the month of July, bound to receive Communion immediately, or may he wait until the following Easter? [51] According to the more common opinion, the child may wait until the Easter season, since it will come within a year of his attaining the use of reason.[52] But the final decision should be left to the pastor. If he should decide that a little more religious instruction is indispensable, then he is within his rights in delaying the reception of the Eucharist for a time.[53] Yet he should keep in mind the warning given by the decree *"Quam Singulari,"* [54] "Even though the children were to prepare for their first Communion by a more serious study—which is not always the case—there would be none the less reason to deplore the loss of their first innocence, which perhaps might have been avoided by the reception of the Eucharist in their tender years."

According to canon 1330, it is also the duty of the pastor to give his best efforts—preferably during Lent, if that is possible—to prepare little children who have come to the use of reason to receive for the first time the Easter Communion to which they are bound in common with the rest of the faithful. The Code does not command the pastor to hold these catechetical instructions during Lent, but it urges him to do so in order to give the children an opportunity to prepare for the fulfilment of the paschal precept.[55]

[51] Cerato, *op. cit.*, p. 12.

[52] Cappello, *De Sacramentis*, I, n. 475.

[53] Canon 859, §1.

[54] Quoted by Cappello, *De Aetate Admittendorum ad Primam Communionem Eucharisticam*, p. 6; *Fontes*, n. 2103.

[55] Cocchi, *Commentarium in Codicem Juris Canonici*, III, p. 43.

CHAPTER V

CIRCUMSTANCES OF THE PRECEPT

ARTICLE I.—THE TIME OF THE PRECEPT

§1. *The Extension of the Paschal Season*

Canon 859. § 2. Paschalis Communio fiat a dominica Palmarum ad dominicam in albis; sed locorum Ordinariis fas est, si ita personarum ac locorum adjuncta exigant, hoc tempus etiam pro omnibus suis fidelibus anticipare, non tamen ante quartam diem dominicam Quadragesimae, vel prorogare, non tamen ultra festum sanctissimae Trinitatis.

FORMERLY it was the practice of the Church to associate the Communion of precept with some great feast. Thus, for example, the Council of Agde commanded that the Eucharist be received on the feasts of Easter, Christmas, and Pentecost. This custom perdured even into the late Middle Ages.[1] After the fourth Lateran Council it happened quite frequently that the faithful who had received absolution in the beginning of Lent, delayed their reception of the Easter Communion until Easter Sunday. Naturally, it soon became impossible for the parish clergy to cope with the vast crowds who were desirous of communicating on this feast.[2] Consequently, local practice and episcopal decrees began to permit the fulfilment of the Easter duty on days other than Easter Sunday.[3] For example, the Council of Avignon [4] ordered that the precept be satis-

[1] Browe, "Die Oesterliche Zeit"—*Theologie und Glaube,* XXI (1929), 345-360.

[2] Browe, *ibid.*

[3] St. Antoninus claimed that the Easter Communion was to be received on Easter Sunday or on one of the two following days. These days he regarded as integral parts of the feast.—*Summa Theologica,* II, p. 995.

[4] *Conc. Avenionen.* (1337), c. IV—Mansi, XXV, 1089.

fied between Palm Sunday and Low Sunday, which is the prescription of the present legislation. This ruling of the Council of Avignon was extended to the whole Church by the declaration of Pope Eugene IV in 1440,[5] and ever since has remained unchanged.

According to canon 859, §2, the Easter season extends from Palm Sunday to Low Sunday, and the common law demands that the paschal precept be satisfied during these two weeks. Hence, if one were to receive Holy Communion even one day before this time, he would not comply with the law, and the obligation to communicate during the paschal time would still remain.[6]

Since these two weeks, because of local conditions, may sometimes be too brief to permit all to satisfy the obligation, the Code grants to Ordinaries the faculty of extending the Easter season for all the faithful of their respective dioceses, from Laetare Sunday to Trinity Sunday, both inclusive.[7] In order that the Ordinary may use this faculty licitly, circumstances of place or person should demand the extension of the Easter time. Local custom or the lack of confessors may be considered as reasonable motives for taking advantage of this concession.[8]

When circumstances arise which make it advisable for the Ordinary to prolong the paschal season, he is not obliged to grant the privilege to the whole diocese. He may grant this extension to one or more of the faithful, or to one or several parishes.[9] It should be noted that pastors cannot extend the Easter time for their parish, although in individual instances they may declare that there is a sufficient reason for a penitent to be exempt from the obligation for the time being.[10]

[5] Ep. "*Fide Digna,*" 8 July 1440—*Fontes,* n. 53.

[6] Provided, of course, that the Ordinary has not extended the time. Cappello, *De Sacramentis,* I, n. 477. Orientals are also bound by the paschal precept as is evident from the first canon in the Code. The Easter season for them, as for the Latins, generally extends from Palm Sunday to Low Sunday. An exception is found in the case of the Egyptian Copts, for whom the time is extended to Pentecost. Cf. Cappello, *op. cit.,* n. 860.

[7] Augustine, *A Commentary,* IV, 238; Vermeersch-Creusen, *Epitome Juris Canonici,* II, 78; Blat, *Commentarium Textus Codicis Juris Canonici,* III, 196.

[8] Vermeersch-Creusen, *op. cit.,* n. 126.

[9] Fanfani, *De Jure Parochorum,* p. 255; Cappello, *op. cit.,* n. 476.

[10] Fanfani, *loc. cit.*

The question has been raised as to the precise meaning of the expression *pro omnibus suis fidelibus,* as found in canon 859. Does it mean that only those who have a domicile or quasi-domicile in a parish or diocese can take advantage of the extension? This is a rather stringent interpretation of the law which does not find favour with authors. It is more correct to hold that the extension of the paschal season can be used not only by all the faithful belonging to the diocese, but also by those who have neither domicile nor quasi-domicile anywhere else, and by those who are at the moment within the confines of the diocese.[11]

The Ordinary may use the faculty granted by the Code provided that there are judicious reasons for the prolongation of the Easter season.[12] But he cannot extend it beyond Laetare Sunday and Trinity Sunday without a special indult.[13] If there are grave reasons for a prolongation beyond the limits allowed by the Code, the Holy See will readily grant special faculties.[14] In the United States, in virtue of a special indult, the Ordinaries were empowered to extend the Easter season from the first Sunday of Lent to Trinity Sunday.[15] Since this indult was granted before the promulgation of the Code, the question was raised as to whether Ordinaries in the United States could still make use of it. Augustine [16] holds that if the indult is considered *as such,* merely as an indult, then by reason of canon four, it is still to be considered as having the force of law. On the other hand, if it is taken as part and parcel of the decrees of the plenary councils, then it is to be looked upon as abrogated by virtue of canon six. The second hypothesis, however, is the less probable because the indult had the force of law, not because of its incorporation in

[11] Cappello, *loc. cit.;* Durieux-Dolphin, *The Eucharist, Law and Practice,* p. 172; Vermeersch-Creusen, *loc. cit.;* Noldin, *De Praeceptis,* 643; Raia, *De Parochis,* p. 110; Prümmer, *Manuale Theologiae Moralis,* III, 158.

[12] Gennari, "Annotazioni," *Il Monitore Ecclesiastico,* IX (1917), 353.

[13] Gennari, *loc. cit.;* Blat, *op. cit.,* III, 196; Noldin, *loc. cit.* Such an indult was given in 1885 to Bishop Perraud of Autun. Cf. *Analecta Ecclesiastica,* V, 541.

[14] Durieux-Dolphin, *The Eucharist, Law and Practice,* p. 172.

[15] Cf. S. C. de Prop. Fide, 16 Oct., 1830; cf. *Coll. Lac.,* III, 36; and *Acta et Decreta Concilii Plenarii Baltimorensis,* II, n. 257.

[16] *Rights and Duties of Ordinaries,* p. 114.

the legislation of the Baltimore councils, but because it was granted by the Holy See. Hence, Ordinaries may still safely use it.

In the event that the bishop grants an extension of the paschal time, whether he does so by virtue of the Code or by reason of special faculties from the Holy See, he must duly promulgate this fact to the faithful.[17] This may be done through the medium of a synodal or particular law,[18] or by publication in the diocesan newspaper, or by any other method the Ordinary may desire to use.

§2. *The Double Obligation*

Canon 859. § 4. Praeceptum paschalis communionis adhuc urget, si quis illud praescripto tempore, quavis de causa, non impleverit.

To understand this prescription of the law, it is of supreme importance to keep in mind that the paschal precept virtually contains a double command, one more general, more essential, partly divine and partly ecclesiastical—that of receiving Holy Communion at least once a year; the other more specific, relatively secondary, although grave, and purely ecclesiastical in origin—that of making this annual Communion during the Easter time.[19] Therefore if any person, whether through deliberate neglect or by reason of circumstances over which he had no control, should omit making his Easter duty during the time specified by the law, there still remains the obligation, binding under pain of mortal sin, of receiving Communion sometime during the year. For, although he can no longer satisfy the secondary obligation of communicating during the Easter season, there still remains the principal obligation of approaching the altar at least once a year.[20]

[17] Augustine, *A Commentary*, p. 238.

[18] Vermeersch-Creusen, *Epitome Juris Canonici*, II, n. 126.

[19] Gasparri, *De SS. Eucharistia*, n. 1157; Cappello, *De Sacramentis*, I, n. 475; Vermeersch-Creusen, *op. cit.*, n. 126.

[20] Cappello, *op. cit.*, n. 478; Gasparri, *op. cit.*, n. 1158; Noldin's explanation of this point is very clear:—"Determinatio temporis apponitur non ad finiendam obligationem, sed ad urgendam observationem."—*De Praeceptis*, p. 643. The same observation was made long before by Benedict XIV, *Institutiones Ecclesiasticae*, XLV, n. 13.

In the event that the Eucharist has not been received within the appointed period, the obligation still remaining does not necessarily have to be satisfied *quam primum*. The law only demands that the Eucharist be received sometime during the year; [21] it does not specify that the precept be satisfied within one week or one month of the completion of the paschal season. Pastors, however, should urge their parishioners to comply with the law as soon as possible,[22] but, at the same time, they must guard against leaving them under the impression that a sin is committed every time an opportunity to receive Communion is neglected.[23]

If the Easter Communion has been neglected during the time appointed for its reception, there still remains the obligation to communicate within the year. How is this year to be computed? Some authors [24] following De Lugo,[25] insist that it may refer to the civil year, so that one who has received Communion during the month of January, has satisfied the divino-ecclesiastical precept for the year. Others [26] claim that it is a question here of the ecclesiastical year which extends from the beginning of one paschal season to the beginning of the next.[27] This second opinion has the greater weight of authority because it is based upon the statement of Pope Eugene IV, namely, "... *sed terminum statuisse a Pascha ad Pascham.*" [28] This epistle is the source of the present discipline on the question of the time within which the paschal precept must be satisfied, and since the Code is silent about the quality of the year, it is reasonable to assume that the declaration of Eugene IV is still valid.[29] How-

[21] De Lugo, *De Sac. Eucharistiae,* disp. XVI, n. 69; Cappello, *op. cit.,* n. 478; Gasparri, *loc. cit.*

[22] Gasparri, *loc. cit.;* Cappello, *loc. cit.*

[23] Durieux-Dolphin, *The Eucharist, Law and Practice,* p. 172.

[24] Vermeersch-Creusen, *Epitome Juris Canonici,* II, n. 126; Genicot-Salsmans, *Institutiones Theologiae Moralis,* II, 180.

[25] *De Sac. Eucharistiae,* disp. XVI, n. 69.

[26] Cappello, *De Sacramentis,* I, n. 475; Raia, *De Parochis,* p. 110; Noldin, *De Praeceptis,* p. 642; Gasparri, *De SS. Eucharistia,* n. 1155.

[27] Gasparri, *loc. cit.*

[28] Ep. "*Fide Digna,*" 8 July 1440—*Fontes,* n. 53.

[29] Cf. Cappello, *loc. cit.;* Noldin, *loc. cit.* On the other hand, Blat holds that the practice of regarding the year as running from Easter to Easter, is not obligatory.—*Commentarium Textus Codicis Juris Canonici,* III, p. 195.

ever, since the former opinion has at least extrinsic probability because of the authorities supporting it, a person is free to take advantage of it. But he must be consistent in using this method of computation, so that one year he cannot choose one method, and the following year, the other, if by so doing he should omit a year.[30]

§3. *Privileges Granted by the Code During the Paschal Season*

> **Canon 859. § 1. Omnis utriusque sexus fidelis . . . nisi forte de consilio proprii sacerdotis, ob aliquam rationabilem causam, ad tempus ab ejus perceptione duxerit abstinendum.**

The Code here repeats verbatim the privilege granted by the Fourth Lateran Council to the *proprius sacerdos* of extending the period designated for the fulfilment of the paschal precept.[31] For some time after the promulgation of the Lateran decree, the phrase, *proprius sacerdos,* was interpreted as meaning only the pastor of the penitent.[32] In course of time, it was understood of any priest who was juridically competent to hear confessions.[33] This is the interpretation accepted today; [34] consequently, every confessor is granted the privilege of advising the penitent to delay for a time the satisfaction of the paschal precept. The word *advising* is used because the Code concedes the faculty of *counselling* the postponement of the Easter Communion only when circumstances warrant it. Gen-

[30] Vermeersch-Creusen, *loc. cit.*

[31] Consequently Kelly in his work, *The Jurisdiction of the Simple Confessor,* p. 192, is incorrect in asserting that the first general concession of this kind was found in the encyclical letter of Benedict XIV, "*Inter Omnigenas,*" 2 Febr. 1744, §21—*Fontes,* n. 339. As a matter of fact, all that Benedict XIV does in this instance, is to extend the paschal season for Serbia from the beginning of Lent to Pentecost, a concession similar to the one which was given to the United States.

[32] Villien, *A History of the Commandments of the Church,* p. 210.

[33] Benedict XIV, *Institutiones Ecclesiasticae,* XLV, n. 6; Many, *Praelectiones de Missa,* p. 306.

[34] Kelly, *The Jurisdiction of the Simple Confessor,* p. 192; Ayrinhac, *Legislation on the Sacraments,* 178; Vermeersch-Creusen, *op. cit.,* n. 126; Gasparri, *op. cit.,* n. 1156.

erally, this privilege should be used only in the confessional, but the confessor may make use of it on occasion even outside the sacramental forum.[35]

The confessor must have some reasonable cause for allowing the postponement of the Easter duty. Furthermore, since he cannot advise such a delay unless it is to the advantage of the penitent (*nisi de re meliori*),[36] it is obvious that the spiritual welfare of the penitent should benefit by the extension of the paschal season. Moralists and canonists of today do not discuss in detail the reasons which would justify a confessor in extending the time for the fulfilment of the paschal precept for a particular penitent. In the past, bodily uncleanness arising from diseases, pollution, menstruation, and marriage obligations were considered sufficient to merit the postponement.[37] Today, a confessor may counsel a penitent, who has been notorious for his evil ways, to put off the fulfilment of the precept for a time in order to avoid possible scandal for the faithful. Or again, if a penitent has serious doubts against the faith, the confessor would do well to advise a delay in the reception of the Easter Communion.[38] As a general rule, the confessor should exercise this prerogative only from a desire to afford the penitent a more perfect preparation, a preparation of which at the moment he is incapable because of his indispositions.

The general purport of canon 859 seems to insinuate that this faculty should be exercised only in exceptional cases.[39] Furthermore, the phrase *ad tempus* indicates that the extension as a rule should be brief; however, if exceptional circumstances warrant it, the time may be extended indefinitely.[40] This does not mean that the penitent should be dispensed from satisfying the obligation altogether; in this whole question the presumption is that the reception of Communion is possible, but at the moment prudence dictates that

[35] Vermeersch-Creusen, *op. cit.*, n. 126.

[36] Vermeersch-Creusen, *loc. cit.*

[37] Browe, "Die oesterliche Zeit,"—*Theologie und Glaube*, Iahrg. 21, 345-360 —quoted in *Apollinaris*, II, 531.

[38] Vermeersch-Creusen, *loc. cit.*

[39] Jombart, "De praevisa ob Missionem ommissione Communionis Paschalis," *Periodica*, XVI (1927), 172.

[40] Kelly, *loc. cit.*

it be deferred. If the fulfilment of the precept were impossible, then the prescriptions of the law would be suspended as long as the impossibility would perdure; under such circumstances, the penitent would not need the permission of the confessor to be excused from complying with the law. But aside from this latter point, the postponement of the reception of the Easter Communion without the permission of the confessor, would be gravely sinful.[41]

If, at the beginning of the year, a person foresees that it will not be possible for him to receive the Eucharist during the paschal season, there is no obligation for him to communicate before that time.[42] Such a Communion would not satisfy the precept, and hence, it is not obligatory. On the other hand, according to the opinion which holds that one may use the civil year for complying with the obligation of the Easter duty, a person can satisfy the primary and principal command of the law, that of communicating once a year,[43] by approaching the altar, for example, during the month of January.

Moralists propose another case which is akin to the preceding one. If a person foresees that circumstances will prevent him from fulfilling the paschal precept later on in the time assigned for this obligation, is he obliged to communicate now if the paschal period has begun? Theologians answer in the affirmative, because the obligation extends to the whole paschal season. If it is foreseen that it will be impossible to satisfy it later on, then one must communicate now when it is possible.[44]

Gasparri [45] makes the assertion that the confessor may permit the anticipation of the Easter Communion, when an impediment will prevent the reception of the Eucharist during the proper period. Such an assertion, however, has no basis in fact, because the pastor or the confessor has no authority to anticipate the paschal Communion. One cannot read into the phrase *ad tempus . . . abstinen-*

[41] Vermeersch-Creusen, *loc. cit.*

[42] Suarez, *Opera Omnia*, disp. LXIX, sect. II, n. 7; De Lugo, *De Sac. Eucharistiae*, disp. XII, n. 74; Cappello, *De Sacramentis*, I, n. 478; Gasparri, *De SS. Eucharistia*, n. 1158.

[43] Vermeersch-Creusen, *Epitome Juris Canonici*, II, n. 126.

[44] Noldin, *De Praeceptis*, n. 693; Genicot-Salsmans, *op. cit.*, p. 208.

[45] *Op. cit.*, n. 1158.

dum a permission to anticipate the Easter season,[46] and since a pastor or confessor cannot dispense from the common law of the Church without express faculties,[47] it is obvious that no justification for such a privilege can be found in canon 859.[48]

> **Canon 899. § 3. Ipso jure a casibus, quos quoquo modo sibi Ordinarii reservaverint, absolvere possunt tum parochi, aliive qui parochorum nomine in jure censentur, toto tempore ad praeceptum paschale adimplendum utili, tum singuli missionarii quo tempore missiones ad populum haberi contingat.**

To facilitate the fulfilment of the paschal precept, the Code grants to pastors, and to those who are equivalent to them in law, the faculty of absolving from episcopal cases during the time in which the Easter duty urges. This power of absolving seems to be ordinary since it is annexed by law to an office bearing with it ordinary jurisdiction for the internal sacramental forum.[49] Not every confessor, it should be noted, can absolve from episcopal cases during the paschal season, but only pastors and those who in the Code are included under the name of pastors. Those who are equivalent to pastors are, quasi-parochi, that is, those in charge of a subdivision of a Vicariate or Prefecture Apostolic, and those who take the place of pastors with full parochial powers.[50]

Since it is the paschal season which is privileged, it follows that any confession made during this time does not have to be made necessarily for the purpose of fulfilling the paschal precept.[51] Nor is this privilege to be limited to the time specified by the common law, because canon 899, §3, expressly mentions that the time is to be considered *tempus utile.* Hence, for example, those to whom this fac-

[46] Jombart, "De praevisa ob Missionem omissione communionis paschalis," *Periodica,* XVI (1927), 173.

[47] Canon 81.

[48] Cappello, *op. cit.,* n. 478.

[49] Dargin, *Reserved Cases according to the Code of Canon Law,* p. 31; Kelly, *The Jurisdiction of the Simple Confessor,* p. 195.

[50] Canon 451, §2.

[51] Vermeersch-Creusen, *op. cit.,* n. 180; Dargin, *op. cit.,* p. 31.

ulty has been granted could use it from the first Sunday of Lent to Trinity Sunday for any confession made during this time in the United States, provided, of course, that the local Ordinary has extended the time. On the other hand, if a confessor, using canon 859, §1, should permit the extension of the paschal period beyond these limits for an individual penitent, a pastor and those included under the name of pastor, could only use this faculty when the confession is being made to fulfill the paschal precept.[52]

Article II.—The Place of the Precept

Canon 859. § 3. Suadendum fidelibus ut huic praecepto satisfaciant in sua quisque paroecia; et qui in aliena paroecia satisfecerint, curent proprium parochum de adimpleto praecepto certiorem facere.

The Fourth Lateran Council did not specify any particular place for the reception of the paschal Communion, but the ancient discipline clearly pointed to the parish church. The parish in olden times formed an almost exclusive society, under somewhat of a feudal constitution, with the faithful as members and the pastor as lord.[53] The whole Christian life was centered around, and emanated from the parochial church; hence it is not surprising that the reception of the Easter Communion came to be considered as a function which should be performed only in one's own parish. Various facts indicate that it was the wish of the Council to have the paschal Communion made in the parish church. For it was the pastor who, as the real *sacerdos proprius* of the Fourth Lateran Council, had received authority to permit a Christian to abstain for a time from compliance with the paschal precept; and it was his office also to turn the negligent away from church and to refuse them Christian burial after death. In course of time, by custom and the explicit approval of the Holy See,[54] it became a general obligation to receive

[52] Kelly, *op. cit.*, p. 196.

[53] Villien, *A History of the Commandments of the Church*, p. 210.

[54] Benedict XIV, ep. encycl. *"Magno cum,"* 2 jun., 1751, §21, 22—*Fontes*, n. 413.

the Easter Communion in the parish church. The rights of the pastor and of the parish church were better maintained with regard to the paschal Communion than with respect to the annual Confession; and even up to beginning of the present century [55] it was regarded as a strict parochial function, and with few exceptions, decisions of the Sacred Congregation of the Council sustained it.[56]

The present dispositions of the Code do not maintain the former discipline, for there is no longer a strict obligation to make the Easter Communion in one's own parish. This is a radical departure from past legislation, but it seems to be in keeping with the general trend of allowing as much freedom as possible to the faithful in matters pertaining to the reception of the Eucharist.[57] However, there are still some vestiges of the old law, because the present legislation favours the reception of the Easter Communion in the home parish, and asks that this practice be recommended to the faithful.

In the event that a person makes his Easter duty in a parish other than the one in which he has his domicile or quasi-domicile, he should notify his proper pastor of this fact.[58] For the pastor still has the right to know his sheep,[59] and since it is his duty to urge the obligation of the paschal precept, he should know whether his parishioners have respected the law of the Church. Although some authors [60] only see in this a mere counsel, it is more correct to hold that the word *curent* indicates a true precept, which however binds only *sub levi.*[61] If the Easter Communion has been received in an

[55] Browe, "Die Kommunion in der Pfarrkirche," *Zeitschrift f. Kath. Theologie,* 53 (1929), 477-516—cited in *Apollinaris,* III (1930), 339.

[56] Since obviously it would be impossible to quote and analyse all the decisions, the references to the Thesaurus will only be given.—Thesaurus Resolutionum S. C. C., II, 104; XI, 45; XIII, 49; XIV, 92; XV, 52; XVIII, 97; XIX, 86; XXI, 73, 91; XLVI, 161, 179; L, 31; LIV, 62, 69, 213; LXIX, 209.

[57] E. g., canon 866. Cf. *Il Monitore Ecclesiastico,* IV, (1922), 157.

[58] Badii, *Institutiones Juris Canonici,* II, n. 363.

[59] Prümmer, *Manuale Theologiae Moralis,* III, n. 212.

[60] Cappello, *De Sacramentis,* I, n. 475; Raia, *De Parochis,* p. 111.

[61] Vermeersch-Creusen, *Epitome Juris Canonici,* II, n. 128; Ayrinhac, *Legislation on the Sacraments,* p. 179; Fanfani, *De Jure Parochorum,* p. 254; Cicognani, *Commentarium ad Librum I Codicis,* p. 339.

oratory or church within the confines of the parish, there is no obligation to inform the pastor. For the Code explicitly states that it is only when the paschal precept has been satisfied in another parish (*in aliena paroecia*) that there is occasion for the notification.

The Code does not discuss the means which the parishioner should use to notify his pastor when the Easter Communion has been made outside the home parish, and authors generally dismiss the matter without comment. Micheletti [62] and Fanfani [63] however, advocate the use of schedules which would testify to the fulfilment of the paschal precept. This is not a new idea, because as early as the seventeenth century it was already recognised that the faithful should have some documentary proof of this very important fact. The use of these *billets de Communion Pascale,* which probably originated in Rome,[64] met with the approval of several diocesan synods.[65]

As Fanfani [66] points out, such a system would be useful today, but it is questionable whether the difficulties of modern conditions would not offset its practicality. It must be remembered that in the seventeenth century the violation of the paschal precept carried with it definite penalties, and consequently it was of supreme importance that the faithful should be able to prove their obedience to this law in order to avoid the sanction. The system of schedules was admirably suited for such a purpose. But the law of annual Communion does not have these penalties today; and this fact coupled with the realisation that there is only a slight obligation to notify the pastor of the making of the Easter duty in another parish, is sufficient to exclude the imposition of a complicated and inconvenient system of schedules upon the parish clergy. Moreover, the individual parishioner will have ample opportunity to inform the pastor of his satis-

[62] *Summula Theologiae Pastoralis,* II, n. 185. Micheletti also gives a facsimile of a certificate used for this purpose in Rome. Cf. p. 11 of the appendix of his work.

[63] *De Jure Parochorum,* p. 255.

[64] "De la Confessione Annuelle et de la Communion Pascale," *Analecta Juris Pontificii* (1860), 2274.

[65] *Ibid.*

[66] *Loc. cit.*

fying the paschal precept outside his parish when the pastor makes his annual visitation of the parish.

ARTICLE III.—THE RITE OF THE PRECEPT

Canon 866. § 1. Omnibus fidelibus cujusvis ritus datur facultas ut, pietatis causa, Sacramentum Eucharistiae quolibet ritu confectum suscipiant.

§ 2. Suadendum tamen ut suo quisque ritu fideles praeceptum communionis paschalis satisfaciant.

§1. *Definition of Terms*

The Latin word *ritus* signifies primarily the form and manner of any religious observance. It may indicate various religious customs, usages, or ceremonies.[67] Considering the term *rite* as understood in Catholic liturgy, it may be defined:—"Ritus stricte significat modum rite actus liturgicos peragendi, seu debitum ordinem externum liturgiae."[68] Accordingly the word *rite* may denote the entire complex of sacred functions or form of liturgy proper to some Church. Thus one may distinguish the Roman rite, the Byzantine rite, etc. *Rite* in canon 866 is to be understood in a restricted sense, that is to say, it refers to any rite provided that it is "Catholic." This connotation designates a group of Catholics who have a proper liturgy for all sacred functions, a proper liturgical language, and are governed by a particular ecclesiastical discipline.[69] The acceptance of the same faith, and the recognition of the supreme jurisdiction of the Pope, are vital and fundamental; hence, theologically all Catholic rites or groups must be in agreement.[70] Generally speaking, all Catholic rites may be divided into two groups, namely, the Latin group and the Oriental. With reference to the Orientals, the term "Catholic rite" designates a group of Oriental Catholics within the

[67] Duskie, *The Canonical Status of the Orientals in the United States*, p. 13.

[68] Wernz-Vidal, *Jus Canonicum*, II, n. 21.

[69] Petrani, *De Relatione Juridica inter Diversos Ritus in Ecclesia Catholica*, p. 1.

[70] Fortescue, *The Uniate Eastern Churches*, pp. 2, 11.

unity of the Catholic fold, who at the same time, have a proper liturgy, a proper liturgical language, and a distinct ecclesiastical discipline.[71]

With these preliminary notions in mind, it will be easier to grasp the full meaning of canon 866. In virtue of this canon, all the faithful of any rite, that is to say, any Catholic rite, are given permission to receive, for reasons of devotion, the Blessed Sacrament consecrated in any rite. All should be urged, however, to receive the Easter Communion in their proper rite.

§2. *Former Discipline*

Even as late as the time of Benedict XIV, in many places where Orientals and Latins lived in one community, there existed the custom of receiving Holy Communion indiscriminately, irrespective of rite.[72] Benedict XIV changed this promiscuous reception of the Eucharist to a large extent. For he prohibited the Latins to receive Holy Communion consecrated according to the Greek rite from the Greek priests. In like manner, the Greeks were forbidden to communicate in the Latin rite, except in a case where they had no churches of their own rite.[73] As a consequence, the practically unrestricted access to Holy Communion in any Catholic rite, as permitted today, was unknown until the latter part of the nineteenth century. Prior to that time, the law demanded that every one receive the Holy Eucharist consecrated with leavened or unleavened bread according to the proper rite of the communicant.[74] This strict discipline was mitigated in 1893 to allow Catholics of any rite to receive Holy Communion at any time from a priest whether he belonged to the Latin or Oriental rite, provided that there was no church or priest of their own rite in the locality.[75] In the follow-

[71] Fortescue, "Rites," *Cath. Encycl.*, XIII, 64-78.

[72] Petrani, *op. cit.*, p. 82.

[73] Benedict XIV, const. *"Etsi Pastoralis,"* 26 Maii, 1742—*Fontes*, n. 328.

[74] Gasparri, *De SS. Eucharistia*, n. 1178; Wernz, *Jus Decretalium*, III, n. 741.

[75] S. Cong. de Prop. Fide, 18 Aug. 1893—*Coll.*, n. 1846. Cf. Petrani, *op. cit.*, p. 85.

ing year it was modified even more, so as to permit the faithful, even where there was a church and priest of their own rite present, to receive the Eucharist in any church, even though the matter of the Sacrament differed, when they were able to attend their proper church because of some grave inconvenience.[76] The purpose of this concession was to obviate the frequent danger to which Catholics were exposed who dwelt in a mixed population and often at great distance from a priest ministering in their own rite, of being prevented from complying with the paschal precept or receiving Holy Communion.[77]

Pius X, in his famous constitution "*Tradita ab Antiquis*,"[78] granted to the faithful the privilege of receiving Holy Communion in any Catholic rite even for devotional motives. He made only one reservation—and that was in the case of the Easter duty. In rule four of this constitution it is stated:—"Quisque fidelium praecepto Communionis satisfaciet, si eam suo ritu accipiat et quidam a parocho suo; cui sane in ceteris obeundis religionis officiis addictus manebit." The Code however has modified this regulation so that a strict obligation has been reduced to a matter of exhortation.

§3. *Present Legislation*

The fact that a Catholic may satisfy the paschal precept by receiving the Eucharist in another rite, is a very practical one. All former legislation, excepting cases of necessity, had firmly insisted that the faithful must satisfy this obligation in their own rite. The wording of the Code, *suadendum est*, still retains some vestige of the old discipline. Although the phrase cannot be interpreted as imposing a precept upon the faithful,[79] still it does not permit the same liberty as is given for the devotional Communion.[80] Two distinct

[76] Leo XIII, litt. ap. "*Orientalium Dignitas*," 30 Nov. 1894—*Fontes*, n. 627.

[77] *A. E. R.*, IX (1894), 70.

[78] Pius X, const. "*Tradita ab Antiquis*," 14 Sept. 1912—*Fontes*, n. 698; *A. A. S.*, IV, 616.

[79] Cicognani, *op. cit.*, p. 338; Cappello, *de Sacramentis*, I, n. 524.

[80] Duskie, *op. cit.*, p. 122.

ideas are embodied in this phrase. First, it insinuates an obligation on the part of those who have the care of souls to exhort the faithful to receive the paschal Communion in their own rite; the Latins in the Latin rite, the Orientals in the Oriental rite.[81] Secondly, it leaves the faithful free to obey or disregard this exhortation.[82] The Church does not favour of a mixture of rites, and this is the principle underlying the admonition of canon 866. However, if a person should deliberately act against the mind of the Church in this matter, he, nevertheless, would satisfy the obligation of the paschal precept, because this exhortation is not compulsory either under pain of ecclesiastical penalty, or of guilt or of sin.[83]

The Code orders the minister of the Eucharist to give Holy Communion either in leavened or unleavened bread, according to the rules of his rite. However, in cases of urgent necessity, when there is no priest of another rite at hand, a priest of an Oriental rite who uses leavened bread, may give Holy Communion in the unleavened form, and a Latin or Oriental priest who uses unleavened bread may give Holy Communion in leavened bread. Each one, however, must observe the ceremonies of his own rite in the manner of giving Holy Communion.[84] What degree of necessity makes it lawful for a Latin priest to administer the Eucharist consecrated with leavened bread, or a Greek to administer the Sacrament consecrated with unleavened bread? It is difficult to make the distinction or draw the line between the various degrees of necessity, but authors agree that this necessity urges if the paschal precept must be fulfilled.[85]

For several years after the promulgation of the Code, it seemed that the Orientals were to be excluded from the mild discipline allowed by canon 866. The Apostolic Delegate to Egypt asked whether this canon (866, §2) abrogated for the Orientals the Constitution of Pius X which required the faithful to make their Easter

[81] Cicognani, *op. cit.*, p. 338.

[82] Cicognani, *ibid.*

[83] Duskie, *op. cit.*, p. 122.

[84] Canon 851.

[85] Duskie, *op. cit.*, p. 118; Woywod, *A Practical Commentary*, I, p. 406; Petrani, *De Relatione Juridica inter Diversos Ritus*, p. 86.

duty in their proper rite. A negative response was given.[86] This meant that the Orientals could not receive the Easter Communion in a Latin rite, and that consequently they did not benefit by the relaxation of the Code on this point. This fact was brought home more forcibly by a later response which stated that in the Orient the faithful were guilty of grave sin and did not discharge their obligation unless they received the Easter Communion in their own rite during the paschal time.[87]

This severe discrimination against the Orientals was removed by a decree of the Congregation for the Oriental Church in 1925, which declared that they also are embraced by the legislation of the Code.[88] The immediate result of this decree was the abrogation of all previous legislation, pontifical or synodal, which was opposed to canon 866. Consequently, the decree *"Cum Episcopo"* [89] which prescribed that the Greek-Ruthenians in the United States receive the Easter Communion in their own rite and from their own pastor, must be considered as no longer having the force of law.[90]

To remove all element of doubt on this point, the Congregation for the Oriental Church issued a new decree for the Greek-Ruthenians in Canada,[91] which was later extended to the United States.[92] This decree allows the reception of the paschal Communion in a Latin rite, with this proviso, however, that the proper pastor must be notified of the fact.[93] If a person necessarily or deliberately complies with the obligation in another rite, prudence demands that this fact be brought to the notice of his proper pastor.

[86] Resp. S. Cong. pro Eccl. Orient. (ad Delegatum Apost. Aegypti). 31 Oct. 1922—apud Cicognani, *op. cit.*, pp. 14, 15.

[87] Resp. S. Cong. pro Eccl. Orient., 24 Aprilis, 1924—apud Cicognani, *loc. cit.*

[88] Decret. S. Cong. pro Eccl. Orient., 26 Jan. 1925, apud Cicognani, *loc. cit.*

[89] S. Cong. de Prop. Fide pro Negotiis, 18 Aug. 1914, art 24—*A. A. S.*, VI (1914), 462.

[90] Vermeersch-Creusen, *Epitome Juris Canonici*, I, n. 49; Cicognani, *op. cit.*, p. 338.

[91] S. C. Pro Ecclesia Orient., decret. 24 Maii, 1930, "De Administratione Ordinariatus Graeco-Rutheni in regione Canadensi."—*A. A. S.*, XXII (1930), 346.

[92] Cf. *A. A. S.*, XXII (1930), 354.

[93] Cap. III, art. 38.

Article IV.—The Sacrilegious Communion

Canon 861.—Praecepto communionis recipiendae non satisfit per sacrilegam communionem.

The Fourth Lateran Council, by the use of the phrase *suscipiens reverenter,* clearly insinuated that the paschal precept could not be satisfied by the reception of a sacrilegious Communion.[94] However, some of the old theologians,[95] disregarding these words of the decree, maintained that a person could satisfy the paschal precept by an unworthy Communion.[96] This opinion was summarily rejected and condemned by Pope Innocent XI,[97] and has likewise been rejected by the Code.

It seems incredible that great theologians like Suarez and De Lugo should have held this opinion, because it is repugnant to good sense that such a Communion should discharge the obligation of the paschal precept. It is evident that Christ ordered the reception of the Eucharist because of the graces which are procured by communicating: these graces, however, are only obtained by the reception of a worthy Communion.[98] Furthermore, their opinion was based upon a wrong interpretation. Granted that the Church cannot prescribe internal acts primarily and directly, still she has the right to prescribe the mode of fulfilling an obligation. For example, she orders that the Divine Office be said *pie et devote.* Since worthiness and

[94] On the other hand, every Communion made during the Easter time, even without the intention of satisfying the precept, fulfils the obligation imposed by the Church. Cf. Gasparri, *De SS. Eucharistia,* n. 1163.

[95] Suarez, *Opera Omnia,* disp. LXX, III, sect. 3; De Lugo, *de Sac. Eucharistiae,* disp. XVI, sect. 4, n. 82.

[96] They base their contention on an analogy drawn from the precept of hearing Mass on Sunday. They claim that, since a person could fulfil this obligation although he is present in the church for some evil purpose, so also a person could satisfy the obligation of the Easter duty by a sacrilegious Communion.

[97] The condemned proposition was: Praecepto communionis annuae satisfit per sacrilegam Domini manducationem.—Prop. 55 dam. 4 March, 1679—*D. B.,* p. 354, n. 1205.

[98] Rosset, *De Eucharistiae Mysterio,* n. 924; Maroto, "De Sancta Eucharistiae Communione."—*Apollinaris,* II (1929), 174.

unworthiness directly affect the manner of receiving the paschal Communion, the Church is entirely within her rights in prescribing its worthy reception.[99]

Therefore, one who has knowingly and willingly made a sacrilegious Communion, must, either before the lapse of the Easter time, or sometime after its expiration, receive the Eucharist worthily in order to comply with the paschal precept.[100]

[99] Rosset, *op. cit.*, n. 925.
[100] Augustine, *A Commentary*, IV, 240.

BIBLIOGRAPHY

Sources

Acta Apostolicae Sedis (*A. A. S.*), Romae, 1909.

Acta et Decreta Conciliorum Recentiorum (*Collectio Lacensis*), 7 vols., Friburgi Brisgoviae, 1870-1890.

Canones et Decreta Concilii Tridentini, 19. ed., Taurini, 1913.

Codex Juris Canonici Pii X Pontificis Maximi jussu digestus Benedicti Papae XV auctoritate promulgatus, Romae, 1918.

Codicis Juris Canonici Fontes, cura Emi. Petri Card. Gasparri editi, 5 vols., Romae, 1925-1930.

Collectanea S. Congregationis de Propaganda Fide, 2 vols., Romae, 1907.

Concilii Plenarii Baltimorensis II (1868), Acta et Decreta, Baltimorae, 1868.

Concilii Plenarii Baltimorensis III (1884), Acta et Decreta, Baltimorae, 1886.

Corpus Juris Canonici, Editio Lipsiensis II (Richter-Friedberg), 2 vols., Lipsiae, 1922.

Ghilardi, J., *Epitome Canonum Conciliorum tum Generalium tum Provincialium ab Apostolis usque ad Annum MDCIX*, 2 vols., Monteregali, 1870.

Hardouin, Jean, *Acta Conciliorum et Epistolae Decretales ac Constitutiones Summorum Pontificum*, 12 vols., Parisiis, 1715.

Mansi, Joannes, *Sacrorum Conciliorum Nova et Amplissima Collectio*, 51 vols., Parisiis, 1901-1927.

Migne, Jacques, *Patrologiae Cursus Completus—Series Latina*, 221 vols. (*M. P. L.*), Parisiis, 1844-1855; *Series Graeca*, 161 vols. (*M. P. L.*), Parisiis, 1858-1864.

Rituale Romanum, ed. typ., Romae, 1925.

Thesaurus Resolutionum Sacrae Congregationis Concilii, 167 vols., Romae, 1718-1908.

Works of Reference

Aertnys-Damen, *Theologia Moralis*, 11. ed., 2 vols., Taurini, 1928.

Alphonsus de Liguori, *Theologia Moralis*, 2 vols., Turoni, 1879.

Augustine, Charles, *A Commentary on the New Code of Canon Law*, 2. ed., 8 vols., St. Louis, 1921-1924.

Augustine, Charles, *Rights and Duties of Ordinaries according to the Code and Apostolic Faculties*, St. Louis, 1924.

Ayrinhac, H. A., *General Legislation in the New Code of Canon Law*, New York, 1923.

Legislation on the Sacraments in the New Code of Canon Law, New York, 1928.

Badii, Caesar, *Institutiones Juris Canonici*, 2 vols., Florentiae, 1921.

Ballerini-Palmieri, *Opus Theologicum Morale*, 7 vols., Prati, 1890.

Barbosa, Augustinus, *Collectanea Doctorum tam Veterumquam Recentiorum in Jus Pontificium Universum*, Lugduni, 1658.

Baumgärtler, Johann, *Die Erstkommunion der Kinder*, München, 1929.

Bellarminus, Robertus, *Opera Omnia ex Editione Veneta, iterum edidit Justinus Fevre*, 12 vols., Parisiis, 1870-1874.

Benedictus XIV, *De Synodo Dioecesana*, 2 vols., Romae, 1806.

—— *Institutiones Ecclesiasticae*, Prati, 1844.

Berardi, Carolus, *Gratiani Canones Genuini ab Apocryphis Discreti, Corrupti ad emendationem Codicum Fidem Exacti, Difficiliores Commoda interpretatione illustrati*, 3 vols. in 4, Venetiis, 1777.

Bingham, Joseph, *Antiquities of the Christian Church*, 2 vols., London, 1856.

Blat, Albertus, *Commentarium Textus Codicis Juris Canonici*, 5 vols., Romae, 1921-1927.

Bona, Joannes, *Rerum Liturgicarum*, Romae, 1671.

Bridgett, T. E., *A History of the Holy Eucharist in Great Britain*, 2 vols., London, 1908.

Cappello, Felix, *De Aetate Admittendorum ad Primam Communionem Eucharisticam*, Romae, 1911.

—— *Tractatus Canonico-Moralis de Sacramentis juxta Codicem Juris Canonici*, 2. ed., 3 vols., Taurinorum-Augustae, 1925.

Catholic Encyclopedia, 17 vols., New York, 1907-1922.

Catechismus Concilii Tridentini, Dijon, 1865.

Cerato, P., *L'agitata Questione sulla età del fanciullo e la Communione di precetto*, Padova, 1924.

Cicognani, Hamletus, *Commentarium ad Librum I Codicis*, Romae, 1925.

Claeys-Bouuaert-Simenon, *Manuale Juris Canonici*, 2. ed., Bandae et Leodii, 1926.

Cocchi, Guidus, *Commentarium in Codicem Juris Canonici*, 2. and 3. ed., 8 vols., Taurinorum Augustae, 1925-1930.

Corblet, Jules, *Histoire du Sacrement del'Eucharistie*, 2 vols., Paris, 1885.

Curran, Charles, *The Eucharistic Life*, New York, 1930.

Dalgairns, J. B., *The Holy Communion*, 3. ed., Dublin, 1868.

D'Annibale, Josephus, *Summula Theologiae Moralis*, 5. ed., 3 vols., Romae, 1908.

Dargin, Edward, *Reserved Cases According to the Code of Canon Law*, Washington, 1924.

De Ledesma, Petrus, *Theologia Moralis*, Tornaci, 1636.

Dens, P., *Tractatus de Sacramento Eucharistiae*, 2. ed., Mechliniae, 1860.

Denziger, H., *Enchiridion Symbolorum et Definitionum*, 9. ed., Lipsiae, 1900.

Devoti, Joannes, *Institutionum Canonicarum Libri IV*, Leodii, 1860.

De Lugo, Joannes, *Disputationes Scholasticae et Morales*, 8 vols., Paris, 1868-1869.

Dictionnaire de Théologie Catholique, 7 vols., 1903-1923.

Döllinger, Joannes, *The First Age of Christianity and the Church,* trans. by Henry Oxenham, London, 1906.

Duchesne, Louis, *Christian Worship—Its Origin and Evolution,* trans. by M. L. McClure, London, 1903.

Durieux, P., *The Eucharist, Law and Practice,* trans. by Rev. Oliver Dolphin, Faribault, 1926.

Duskie, John, *The Canonical Status of the Orientals in the United States,* Washington, 1928.

Fagnanus, Prosperus, *Commentarium in Libros Decretalium,* Venetiis, 1729.

Fanfani, Ludovicus, *De Jure Parochorum ad Normam Codicis Juris Canonici,* Taurini-Rame, 1924.

Ferraris, Lucius, *Bibliotheca canonica juridica moralis theologica nec non ascetica polemica rubricistica historica,* 9 vols., Romae, 1889.

Ferreres, Joannes, *Compendum Theologiae Moralis,* 7. ed., 2 vols., Barcinone, 1928.

—— *Institutiones Canonicae juxta Novissimum Codicem Pii X a Benedicto XV promulgatum juxtaque praescripta Hispanae Disciplinae et Americae Latinae,* 2 vols., Barcinone, 1918.

Fortescue, Adrian, *The Uniate Eastern Churches,* London, 1923.

Fouard, C., *St. Paul and His Missionary Journeys,* trans. by Griffiths, F., New York, 1894.

Gasparri, Petrus, *Tractatus de Sanctissima Eucharistia,* 3. ed., 2 vols., Parisiis et Lugduni, 1897.

Genicot-Salsmans, *Institutiones Theologiae Moralis,* 11. ed., 2 vols., Bruxellis, 1927.

Gennari, Casimiro, *Sulla Età della prima Communione dei Fanciulli,* 2. ed., Roma, 1910.

Hedley, John Cuthbert, *The Holy Eucharist,* London, 1923.

Hefele, Carl Joseph von, *Conciliengeschichte,* 2. ed., 9 vols., Freiburg, 1873-1890.

Jorio, Domenico, *La Communione Agl' Infermi—Note pratiche di Disciplina Sacramentale,* Roma, 1931.

Kelly, James Patrick, *The Jurisdiction of the Simple Confessor,* Washington, 1927.

Koudelka, Charles, *Pastors, Their Rights and Duties According to the New Code of Canon Law,* Washington, 1921.

Labauche, L., *The Three Sacraments of Initiation,* authorized translation, New York, 1922.

Lupi, Davide, *La SS. Eucaristia, Sacramento e Sacrificio,* Torino-Roma, 1924.

Many, S., *Praelectiones de Missa cum Appendice de SS. Eucharistiae Sacramento,* Paris, 1903.

Micheletti, Am., *Summula Theologiae Pastoralis,* 2. ed., 3 vols., Romae, 1924.

Moran, P. F., *Essays on the Origin, Doctrines, and Discipline of the Early Irish Church,* Dublin, 1864.

Mothon, Joseph, *Institutions Canoniques,* 3 vols., Bruges, 1924.

Noldin, H., *Summa Theologiae Moralis*, 18. ed., 3 vols., Oeniponte, 1926.
O'Brien, John, *A History of the Mass*, 15. ed., New York, 1879.
Perez, P. Raphael, *Decisiones Pontificiae ad Canones Codicis Juris Canonici*, Regalis Monasterii Escurialensis, 1928.
Petrani, Alexius, *De Relatione Juridica inter diversos Ritus in Ecclesia Catholica*, Taurini-Romae, 1930.
Pohle, J., *The Sacraments*, trans. by Arthur Preuss, 7 vols., St. Louis, 1920.
Probst, Ferdinand, *Sakramente und Sakramentalien in den drei ersten Christlichen Jahrhunderten*, Tübingen, 1872.
Pruemmer, Dom., *Manuale Juris Canonici*, 4. et 5. ed., Friburgi Brisgoviae, 1927.
—— *Manuale Theologiae Moralis*, 2. ed., 3 vols., Friburgi Brisgoviae, 1923.
Raia, Salvatore, *De Parochis, De Vicariis Paroecialibus, de Ecclesiarum Rectoribus*, Romae, 1921.
Rauschen, Gerhard, *Eucharist and Penance in the First Six Centuries*, authorized translation, St. Louis, 1913.
Rosset, M., *Theologia Dogmatica-Moralis*, Camberii, 1876.
Schmitz, Herm., *Die Bussbücher und die Bussdisciplin der Kirche*, Mainz, 1883.
Schulze, Frederick, *Manual of Pastoral Theology*, 6. ed., St. Louis, 1929.
Suarez, Franciscus, *Opera Omnia*, 26 vols., Parisiis, 1856.
Tanquerey, Ad., *Synopsis Theologiae Dogmaticae*, 20. ed., 3 vols., Romae, 1926.
Thomas Aquinas, *Summa Theologica*, 2. ed., Romae, 1894.
Van Espen, Zezerus, *Jus Ecclesiasticum Universum*, Venetiis, 1769.
Vermeersch, Arturus, *Theologia Moralis, Principia, Responsa, Consilia*, 3 vols., Romae, 1923.
Vermeersch-Creusen, *Epitome Juris Canonici cum Commentariis ad Scholas et ad Usum Privatum*, 4. ed., 3 vols., Romae, 1930.
Villien, A., *A History of the Commandments of the Church*, authorized translation, St. Louis, 1915.
Waterworth, *Canons and Decrees of the Council of Trent*, London, 1848.
Wernz, Franciscus, *Jus Decretalium ad Usum Praelectionum in Scholis Textus Canonici sive Juris Decretalium*, 6 vols., Prati, 1915.
Wernz-Vidal, *Jus Canonicum*, 3 vols., Romae, 1923-1927.
Woywod, Stanislaus, *A Practical Commentary on the Code of Canon Law*, 2 vols., New York, 1926.
Zulueta, F. M., *Early First Communion*, London, 1911.

Periodicals

American Ecclesiastical Review, The (*A. E. R.*), Philadelphia, 1889.—
Analecta Ecclesiastica, Romae, 1893-1911.
Analecta Juris Pontificii, Romae, 1860-1861.
Archiv für katholisches Kirchenrecht (*AkKR*), Innsbruck, 1857.—
Apollinaris, Romae, 1928.—

Il Monitore Ecclesiastico, Romae, 1888.—
Irish Ecclesiastical Record (*I. E. R.*), Dublin, 1864.—
Jus Pontificium, Romae, 1921.—
Nouvelle Revue Théologique, Paris, 1856.—
Periodica, de Re Canonica et Morali, Romae et Brugis, 1905.—
Perfice Munus, Torino, 1926.—
Razon y Fe, Madrid, 1901.—

Universitas Catholica Americae

WASHINGTON, D. C.

Facultas Juris Canonici

No. 73

1932

DEUS LUX MEA

TITULI

QUOS

AD DOCTORATUS GRADUM

IN

JURE CANONICO

APUD UNIVERSITATEM CATHOLICAM AMERICAE

CONSEQUENDUM

PUBLICE PROPUGNABIT

CONNELLUS CLINTON

SACERDOS ARCHIDIOECESIS PHILADELPHIENSIS

JURIS CANONICI LICENTIATUS

HORA IX, A. M. DIE XIX MAII MCMXXXII

TITULI

IN IURE CANONICO

I.	De Dissertatione.	
II.	De Historia Iuris Canonici.	
III.	Canones 1-7	De Ambitu Codicis.
IV.	Canones 8-24	De Legibus Ecclesiasticis.
V.	Canones 25-30	De Consuetudine.
VI.	Canones 31-35	De Temporis Supputatione.
VII.	Canones 36-62	De Rescriptis.
VIII.	Canones 63-79	De Privilegiis.
IX.	Canones 80-86	De Dispensationibus.
X.	Cannoes 87-107	Generales Notiones de Personis.
XI.	Canones 111-117	De Clericorum Adscriptione Alicui Dioecesi.
XII.	Canones 118-123	De Iuribus et Privilegiis Clericorum
XIII.	Canones 124-144	De Obligationibus Clericorum.
XIV.	Canones 145-195	De Officiis Ecclesiasticis.
XV.	Canones 196-210	De Potestate Ordinaria et Delegata.
XVI.	Canones 487-498	De Notione Religionis, et de Erectione et Suppressione Religionis, Provinciae, Domus.
XVII.	Canones 499-537	De Religionum Regimine.
XVIII.	Canones 538-586	De Admissione in Religionem.
XIX.	Canones 673-681	De Societatibus sive Virorum sive Mulierum in Communi Viventium sine Votis.
XX.	Canones 1012-1018	De Matrimonio in Genere.
XXI.	Canones 1019-1034	De Iis quae Matrimonii Celebrationi Praemitti debent.
XXII.	Canones 1035-1057	De Impedimentis in Genere.
XXIII.	Canones 1058-1066	De Impedimentis Impedientibus.
XXIV.	Canones 1067-1080	De Impedimentis Dirimentibus.
XXV.	Canones 1081-1093	De Consensu Matrimoniali.
XXVI.	Canones 1552-1568	De Notione Iudicii et de Foro Competenti.
XXVII.	Canones 1569-1607	De Variis Tribunalium Gradibus et Speciebus.
XXVIII.	Canones 1608-1645	De Disciplina in Tribunalibus Servanda.
XXIX.	Canones 1646-1666	De Partibus in Causa.
XXX.	Canones 1667-1705	De Actionibus et Exceptionibus.
XXXI.	Canones 1706-1725	De Causae Introductione.
XXXII.	Canones 1726-1746	De Litis Contestatione, de Litis Instantia, et de Interrogationibus Partibus in Iudicio Faciendis.
XXXIII.	Canones 1747-1836	De Probationibus.
XXXIV.	Canones 1837-1857	De Causis Incidentibus.

XXXV.	Canones 1858-1877	De Processus Publicatione, de Conclusione in Causa, de Causae Discussione, et de Sententia.
XXXVI.	Canones 1879-1891	De Appellatione.
XXXVII.	Canones 1902-1907	De Re Iudicata et de Restitutione in Integrum.
XXXVIII.	Canones 1960-1992	De Causis Matrimonialibus.
XXXIX.	Canones 2195-2198	De Natura Delicti eiusque Divisione.
XL.	Canones 2199-2211	De Imputabilitate Delicti, de Causis illam Aggravantibus vel Minuentibus, et de Iuridicis Delicti Effectibus.
XLI.	Canones 2212-2213	De Conatu Delicti.
XLII.	Canones 2214-2240	De Poenis in Genere.
XLIII.	Canones 2241-2285	De Poenis Medicinalibus seu de Censuris.
XLIV.	Canones 2286-2305	De Poenis Vindicativis.
XLV.	Canones 2306-2313	De Remediis Poenalibus et Poenitentiis.

IN IURE ROMANO

XLVI. The Periods of Roman Law.
XLVII. The Sources of Roman Law.
XLVIII. Personality.
XLIX. Slavery.
L. Citizenship.
LI. Patria Potestas.
LII. Personae in Manu.
LIII. Tutela et Cura.
LIV. Personae in Mancipio.
LV. Ownership.

AMERICAN CHURCH CIVIL LAW

LVI. Tax Exemption.
LVII. Trusts.
LVIII. Marriage.
LIX. Christian Burial.
LX. Wills.

Vidit Facultas:

VALENTINUS T. SCHAAF, O.F.M., J.C.D., Vice-Decanus.
LUDOVICUS H. MOTRY, S.T.D., J.C.D., a Secretis.
FRANCISCUS J. LARDONE, S.T.D., J.U.D.

Vidit Rector Magnificus Universitatis:

JACOBUS HUGO RYAN, S.T.D., PH.D., LL.D., LITT.D.

BIOGRAPHICAL NOTE

CONNELL CLINTON was born April 1, 1907, at Donegal, County Donegal, Ireland. He received his secondary education at St. Eunan's College, Letterkenny, County Donegal, from which he matriculated for the National University of Ireland in June, 1924. His philosophical and theological studies were made at St. Charles' Seminary, Overbrook, Pennsylvania, from which institution he received the degree of Bachelor of Arts. In the fall of 1930 he entered the Catholic University to pursue a graduate course of studies in Canon Law. He was ordained to the Holy Priesthood on May 30, 1931.

CANON LAW STUDIES

1. FRERIKS, REV. CELESTINE A., C.PP.S., J.C.D., Religious Congregations in Their External Relations, 121 pp., 1916.
2. GALLIHER, REV. DANIEL M., O.P., J.C.D., Canonical Elections, 117 pp., 1917.
3. BORKOWSKI, REV. AURELIUS L., O.F.M., De Confraternitatibus Ecclesiasticis, 136 pp., 1918.
4. CASTILLO, REV. CAYO, J.C.D., Disertacion Historico-canonica sobre la Potestad del Cabildo en Sede Vacante o Impedida del Vicario Capitular, 99 pp., 1919 (1918).
5. KUBELBECK, REV. WILLIAM J., S.T.B., J.C.D., The Sacred Penitentiaria and Its Relations to Faculties of Ordinaries and Priests, 129 pp., 1918.
6. PETROVITS, REV. JOSEPH J. C., S.T.D., J.C.D., The New Church Law on Matrimony, X-461 pp., 1919.
7. HICKEY, REV. JOHN J., S.T.B., J.C.D., Irregularities and Simple Impediments in the New Code of Canon Law, 100 pp., 1920.
8. KLEKOTKA, REV. PETER J., S.T.B., J.C.D., Diocesan Consultors, 179 pp., 1920.
9. WANNENMACHER, REV. FRANCIS, J.C.D., The Evidence in Ecclesiastical Procedure Affecting the Marriage Bond, 1920. (Not Printed.)
10. GOLDEN, REV. HENRY FRANCIS, J.C.D., Parochial Benefices in the New Code, IV-119 pp., 1921. (Printed 1925.)
11. KOUDELKA, REV. CHARLES J., J.C.D., Pastors, Their Rights and Duties According to the New Code of Canon Law, 211 pp., 1921.
12. MELO, REV. ANTONIUS, O.F.M., J.C.D., De Exemptione Regularium, X-188 pp., 1921.
13. SCHAAF, REV. VALENTINE THEODORE, O.F.M., S.T.B., J.C.D., The Cloister, X-180 pp., 1921.
14. BURKE, REV. THOMAS JOSEPH, S.T.B., J.C.D., Competence in Ecclesiastical Tribunals, IV-117 pp., 1922.
15. LEECH, REV. GEORGE LEO, J.C.D., A Comparative Study of the Constitution "Apostolicae Sedis" and the "Codex Juris Canonici," 179 pp., 1922.
16. MOTRY, REV. HUBERT LOUIS, S.T.D., J.C.D., Diocesan Faculties according to the Code of Canon Law, II-167 pp., 1922.
17. MURPHY, REV. GEORGE LAWRENCE, J.C.D., Delinquencies and Penalties in the Administration and the Reception of the Sacraments, IV-121 pp., 1923.
18. O'REILLY, REV. JOHN ANTHONY, S.T.B., J.C.D., Ecclesiastical Sepulture in the New Code of Canon Law, II-129 pp., 1923.
19. MICHALICKA, REV. WENCESLAS CYRILL, O.S.B., J.C.D., Judicial Procedure in Dismissal of Clerical Exempt Religious, 107 pp., 1923.
20. DARGIN, REV. EDWARD VINCENT, S.T.B., J.C.D., Reserved Cases According to the Code of Canon Law, IV-103 pp., 1924.
21. GODFREY, REV. JOHN A., S.T.B., J.C.D., The Right of Patronage According to the Code of Canon Law, 153 pp., 1924.
22. HAGEDORN, REV. FRANCIS EDWARD, J.C.D., General Legislation on Indulgences, II-154 pp., 1924.

23. King, Rev. James Ignatius, J.C.D., The Administration of the Sacraments to Dying Non-Catholics, V-141 pp., 1924.
24. Winslow, Rev. Francis Joseph, A.F.M., J.C.D., Vicars and Prefects Apostolic, IV-149 pp., 1924.
25. Correa, Rev. Jose Servelion, S.T.L., J.C.D., La Potestad Legislativa de la Iglesia Católica, IV-127 pp., 1925.
26. Dugan, Rev. Henry Francis, M.A., J.C.D., The Judiciary Department of the Diocesan Curia, 87 pp., 1925.
27. Keller, Rev. Charles Frederick, S.T.B., J.C.D., Mass Stipends, 167 pp., 1925.
28. Paschang, Rev. John Linus, J.C.D., The Sacramentals According to the Code of Canon Law, 129 pp., 1925.
29. Piontek, Rev. Cyrillus, O.F.M., S.T.B., J.C.D., De Indulto Exclaustrationis necnon Saecularizationis, XIII-289 pp., 1925.
30. Kearney, Rev. Richard Joseph, S.T.B., J.C.D., Sponsors at Baptism According to the Code of Canon Law, IV-127 pp., 1925.
31. Bartlett, Rev. Chester Joseph, A.M., LL.B., J.C.D., The Tenure of Parochial Property in the United States of America, V-108 pp., 1926.
32. Kilker, Rev. Adrian Jerome, J.C.D., Extreme Unction, V-425 pp., 1926.
33. McCormick, Rev. Robert Emmett, J.C.D., Confessors of Religious, VIII-266 pp., 1926.
34. Miller, Rev. Newton Thomas, J.C.D., Founded Masses According to the Code of Canon Law, VII-93 pp., 1926.
35. Roelker, Rev. Edward G., S.T.D., J.C.D., Principles of Privilege According to the Code of Canon Law, XI-166 pp., 1926.
36. Bakalarczyk, Rev. Richardus, M.I.C., J.U.D., De Novitiatu, VIII-208 pp., 1927.
37. Pizzuti, Rev. Lawrence, O.F.M., J.U.L., De Parochis Religiosis, 1927. (Not Printed.)
38. Bliley, Rev. Nicholas Martin, O.S.B., J.C.D., Altars According to the Code of Canon Law, XIX-132 pp., 1927.
39. Brown, Brendan Francis, A.B., LL.M., J.U.D., The Canonical Juristic Personality with Special Reference to its Status in the United States of America, V-212 pp., 1927.
40. Cavanaugh, Rev. William Thomas. C.P., J.U.D., The Reservation of the Blessed Sacrament, VIII-101 pp., 1927.
41. Doheny, Rev. William J., C.S.C., A.B., J.U.D., Church Property: Modes of Acquisition, X-118 pp., 1927.
42. Feldhaus, Rev. Aloysius H., C.PP.S., J.C.D., Oratories, IX-141 pp., 1927.
43. Kelly, Rev. James Patrick, A.B., J.C.D., The Jurisdiction of the Simple Confessor, X-208 pp., 1927.
44. Neuberger, Rev. Nicholas J., J.C.D., Canon 6 or the Relation of the Codex Juris Canonici to the Preceding Legislation, V-95 pp., 1927.
45. O'Keeffe, Rev. Gerald Michael, J.C.D., Matrimonial Dispensations, Powers of Bishops, Priests, and Confessors, VIII-232 pp., 1927.
46. Quigley, Rev. Joseph, A.M., A.B., J.C.D., Condemned Societies, 139 pp., 1927.
47. Zaplotnik, Rev. Ioannes Leo, J.C.D., De Vicariis Foraneis, X-142 pp., 1927.

48. Duskie, Rev. John Aloysius, A.B., J.C.D., The Canonical Status of the Orientals in the United States, VIII-196 pp., 1928.
49. Hyland, Rev. Francis Edward, J.C.D., Excommunication, Its Nature, Historical Development and Effects, VIII-181 pp., 1928.
50. Reinmann, Rev. Gerald Joseph, O.M.C., J.C.D., The Third Order Secular of Saint Francis, 201 pp., 1928.
51. Schenk, Rev. Francis J., J.C.D., The Matrimonial Impediments of Mixed Religion and Disparity of Cult, XVI-318 pp., 1929.
52. Coady, Rev. John Joseph, S.T.D., J.U.D., A.M., The Appointment of Pastors, VIII-150 pp., 1929.
53. Kay, Rev. Thomas Henry, J.C.D., Competence in Matrimonial Procedure, VIII-164 pp., 1929.
54. Turner, Rev. Sidney Joseph, C.P., J.U.D., The Vow of Poverty, XLIX-217 pp., 1929.
55. Kearney, Rev. Raymond A., A.B., S.T.D., J.C.D., The Principles of Delegation, VII-149 pp., 1929.
56. Conran, Rev. Edward James, A.B., J.C.D., The Interdict, V-163 pp., 1930.
57. O'Neil, Rev. William H., J.C.D., Papal Rescripts of Favor, VII-218 pp.,
58. Bastnagel, Rev. Clement Vincent, J.U.D., The Appointment of Parochial Adjutants and Assistants, XV-257 pp., 1930.
59. Ferry, Rev. William A., A.B., J.C.D., Stole Fees, X-107 pp., 1930.
60. Costello, Rev. John Michael, A.B., J.C.D., Domicile and Quasi-Domicile, VII-201 pp., 1930.
61. Kremer, Rev. Michael Nicholas, A.B., S.T.B., J.C.D., Church Support in the United States, VI-136 pp., 1930.
62. Angulo, Rev. Luis, C.M., J.C.D., Legislación de la Iglesia sobre la intención en la aplicación de la Santa Misa, VII-104 pp., 1931.
63. Frey, Rev. Wolfgang Norbert, O.S.B., A.B., J.C.D., The Act of Religious Profession, VIII-174 pp., 1931.
64. Roberts, Rev. James Brendan, A.B., J.C.D., The Banns of Marriage, XIV-140 pp., 1931.
65. Ryder, Rev. Raymond Aloysius, A.B., J.C.D., Simony, IX-151 pp., 1931.
66. Campagna, Rev. Angelo, Ph.D., J.U.D., Il Vicario Generale del Vescovo, VII-205 pp., 1931.
67. Cox, Rev. Joseph Godfrey, A.B., J.C.D., The Administration of Seminaries, VI-124 pp., 1931.
68. Gregory, Rev. Donald J., J.U.D., The Pauline Privilege, XV-165 pp., 1931.
60. Donohue, Rev. John F., J.C.D., The Impediment of Crime, VIII-110 pp., 1931.
70. Dooley, Rev. Eugene A., O.M.I., J.C.D., Church Law on Sacred Relics, IX-143 pp., 1931.
71. Orth, Rev. Clement Raymond, O.M.C., J.C.D., The Approbation of Religious Institutes, 171 pp., 1931.
72. Pernicone, Rev. Joseph M., A.B., J.C.D., The Ecclesiastical Prohibition of Books, XII-267 pp., 1932.
73. Clinton, Rev. Connell, A.B., J.C.L., The Paschal Precept, 1932.
74. Donnelly, Rev. Francis B., A.M., S.T.L., J.C.L., The Diocesan Synod, 1932.

75. TORRENTE, REV. CAMILO, C.M.F., J.C.L., Las Processiones Sagradas, 1932.
76. MURPHY, REV. EDWIN J., C.PP.S., J.C.L., Suspension Ex Informata Conscientia, 1932.
77. MACKENZIE, REV. ERIC F., A.M., S.T.L., J.C.L., The Delict of Heresy in its Commission, Penalization, Absolution, 1932.
78. LYONS, REV. AVITUS E., S.T.B., J.C.L., The Collegiate Tribunal of First Instance, 1932.
79. CONNOLLY, REV. THOMAS A., J.C.L., Appeals, 1932.
80. SANGMEISTER, REV. JOSEPH V., A.B., J.C.L., Force and Fear as Precluding Matrimonial Consent, 1932.
81. JAEGER, REV. LEO A., A.B., J.C.L., The Administration of Vacant and Quasi-Vacant Episcopal Sees in the United States, 1932.
82. RIMLINGER, REV. HERBERT T., J.C.L., Error Invalidating Matrimonial Consent, 1932.
83. BARRETT, REV. JOHN D. M., S.S., J.C.L., Comparative Study of the Third Plenary Council and the Code, 1932.

www.ingramcontent.com/pod-product-compliance
Lightning Source LLC
LaVergne TN
LVHW050202080826
844660LV00012B/336